AUTHOR

Behind The
Locked Door

AUTISM

Behind The Locked Door

Understanding My Life as an Autistic

By Paul Louden

Library of Congress Cataloging-in-Publication Data is available.

ISBN 978-0-9982550-0-2

ISBN 978-0-9982550-1-9 (ebook)

For Ray, Ash, Mom and Dad.Without you, this wouldn't have happened." and then "Special thanks to Sharon Spoonemore, Sondra Hicks, and DWPR for helping me take my thoughts and make them into a book.

ABOUT THE AUTHOR

Paul Louden is a renowned autism expert, advocate for the neuroatypical, public speaker, and radio host. Growing up with troubling issues that confounded both his parents and himself, he finally had some of his life questions answered when he was diagnosed with autism at the age of twenty-three. As a result, he has a unique perspective on adult treatments for autism spectrum disorder, and strives daily to make the discussion of mental health issues less stigmatized and more accepted.

On his Theories of Mind radio show that is broadcast weekly throughout the Houston, Texas area and is available on global podcast, Louden is able to detail the challenges he and others on the autism spectrum face in their lives on a daily and long-term basis. His popularity in the neuroatypical community has led to him being featured in Autism World magazine, copresenting parent training programs in the U.S. and abroad, and being interviewed multiple times for television.

Louden is also a highly sought-after speaker in autism communities, corporate environments, and school settings for his ability to elaborate on the autistic mind. He advocates for those on the autism spectrum who are not well understood or fully accepted by society at large. A forward-thinker, he specializes in discussing the melding of technology with special needs.

Louden lives in the Houston suburb of Spring, Texas and can be reached via his website at *www.loudenonautism.com,* via his email at *theoriesofmindradio@gmail.com,* or through his Facebook page at *www.facebook.com/theoriesofmind.*

Table of Contents

FOREWORD

When I first met Paul Louden in 2006, I had no idea the profound impact he would have on my life. For nine years leading up to that encounter, I had been in the field of Autism Spectrum Disorders (ASD), working with individuals from age two through well into their fifties.

Paul immediately stood out significantly from most of the other individuals on the spectrum that I had worked with in that he had—and continues to have—a unique ability to articulate accurate insight into the real-life challenges of living with autism. Added to that was a passion for helping others that has grown enough to inspire him to write this book.

Most young people struggle with the issues of life, but those with autism have greater obstacles to overcome, and Paul was no exception. Though he grew up in a supportive household, his atypical responses to different situations went either undiagnosed or misdiagnosed, and the word "autism" was never mentioned. It wasn't until he was twenty-three years old that he received the accurate diagnosis of autism, answering many of the questions that had plagued both him and his family over the years.

Our first meeting was shortly after that diagnosis. He came to me with a severe lack of motivation, withdrawal, depression, resistance, mistrust, and despair. He had dropped out of college and was unable to hold down a job. For Team Louden—consisting primarily of Paul, his parents, and myself—our work was cut out for us. But in time, Paul made his way to a place of active participation in his own growth and development. The journey was neither easy nor overnight; if it was, there wouldn't be the ongoing issues with understanding—or, to be more precise, misunderstanding— of autism that inspired Paul to reach out to help as many others on the spectrum as he could.

As Paul's evolution continued, as fraught with setbacks and hurdles as it often was, the small steps of progress became long strides of success. Team Louden was resilient and determined, and Paul grew to be someone with a greater sense of self-awareness, and an even greater awareness of the needs of others. And that is when he changed from student patient to advocate.

Paul chose radio as his first medium to get the word out to audiences who were both on the spectrum and who were neurotypical. His inaugural radio series, *Understanding Autism,* which I had the privilege to cohost with him, premiered in 2011, catering to markets in Houston, Texas and Phoenix, Arizona, and gained enough traction for him to start a new radio series, Theories of Mind, in late 2014. Theories of Mind currently runs weekly on a local Houston radio station and on podcast. His experiences on the radio show prompted him to reach an even greater audience with a mass-produced book. And here we are today.

Understanding a loved one on the spectrum can be an overwhelming experience for parents and professionals and public alike. Daily interactions can be a struggle for all concerned. While there are many resources available for parents in the local bookstore or support group, the greatest resource is often overlooked: the parents' own autistic child. Who better to teach parents about autism than someone with autism?

Paul has great expertise in the area of providing insights into the many challenges that come with processing differences. The stories he shares in this book are personal, insightful, and thought-provoking. Anyone reading this book will come away with a new perspective and clearer way of thinking of how to better relate to loved ones—and even strangers—with autism.

Paul Louden is the new voice of advocacy for autism awareness. I know all will benefit from his stories and insight.

Kimberly Isaac-Emery, M.Sc.
Autism Spectrum Disorder Specialist
Certified Relationship Development Intervention™ Consultant

CHAPTER 1
Introduction:
OUT OF THE
DARKNESS

"Paul Louden, an autistic adult, bravely shares personal narratives to bridge understanding between those with autism and those without. With compelling detail, Paul invites those wired neuro-typically into his autistic experiences. Paul tackles tough stuff such as motivation for hygiene, difficulty sustaining family bonds and differences in emotional memory.
He shares hidden aspects of daily life with clarity, courage and humor. In doing so, readers discover a respect for neurological differences. This book is more than a how-to manual; the material within allows others to create their own personalized road-map toward more empathic responses, better interactions, and deeper understanding of each other. Anecdotes from Paul and his parents provide an understanding of what it means to live with someone with a neurology different than your own. Paul recognizes both personal strengths and struggles. In doing so, it becomes clear that autistic wiring does not change one's need for genuine connections, a sense of belonging, and a desire to be understood. This is a must-read."

Jenny Palmiotto, Psy. D., Founder, Love & Autism

"What do I do?" I asked my mom as I looked at the playground. I was four years old. "Go swing, or go down the slide," she responded. I did as I had been told, then returned to ask, "Now what?" I liked the swing and I liked the slide, but that enjoyment didn't really push me to want to do it again and initiate myself. The past experience of enjoying it just wasn't driving action.

When I played with toys, I limited myself to the "right" way. If a piece was missing from a set, I wouldn't fill in a similar one. I wouldn't use my imagination to fill in gaps, or view the toys as real cars and airplanes. I didn't pretend to be an adult, let alone some more fictional role like a superhero. I hardly understood playing with others or got much out of it—I simply couldn't understand what they were thinking.

When I did invite someone over, it was for a purpose. They were here to play a specific game, or do a specific activity. The rules were to be followed to the letter: No variations, no improvisations. When we were done, we were done, time for them to leave. This hardly changed as I grew older. Even in high school, if a friend had come to watch a movie or play videogames, I often was ready for them to leave once planned activities were over.

For twenty-two years I went through life experiencing the world and the motions both of myself and those around me in a very different way than others do. Meanwhile, every few years I found myself in a new school with new kids to fail to befriend. I often just buried my nose in a book, and the difficulties were attributed to the frequent changes in our lives, and my difficulty adjusting to them.

I didn't really understand friendship the way others did. I shared activities with people, but it often didn't connect to me that it matters so much which people I was sharing those activities with. If I ran into someone I knew, it wouldn't really occur to me to speak up or call out—they were just another person out in the world if not part of a planned activity. If they spoke to me, there would often be a severe impatience to get back to what I was doing and no real desire to catch up or bond socially.

Despite my challenges, I managed to graduate from high school normally at eighteen with no repeated grades or significant academic failures, though I repeated a year of Spanish and squeaked by in a few other classes. I did excellently on my AP exams and had a nearly perfect SAT score missing just one question. With these I felt prepared, and went off to college. By twenty-two I'd failed twice to graduate from college, had similar luck with employment, suffered from recurring bouts of severe depression and generally found myself unable to come to terms with navigating the world around me. I was unable to manage my own life, and saw little chance of gaining control of it.

By chance, during this time I read an article about the odd behavior of a public figure, and how it might represent a condition known as Asperger's syndrome. I can't remember who it was about, where I read the article, or even precisely how I happened to stumble across it. Yet, as I read the article I found myself relating more and more to the descriptions of this person, and the kind of reasoning that leads an Asperger's individual to behave that way. He didn't have a diagnosis, at least not publicly, and neither did I, but now I thought one might be warranted. I felt I had a starting place, and a little bit of hope.

As soon as I finished the article, I forwarded it to my parents. I didn't want to research too much about Asperger's for fear of attempting to fit myself to the symptoms, and instead left it to those who had been observing from the outside to see if my idea made any sense. After reading the article, they saw something there too, and we found a neuropsychologist with experience in autism to perform testing and potentially provide a diagnosis. After written tests, IQ tests, hearing tests, in-depth questions about past behavior for my parents as well as myself, and more I'm sure I no longer remember, we eventually received a diagnosis of Asperger's syndrome.

Asperger's syndrome is a developmental disorder on the autism spectrum, and as such is defined in part by impairments in social communication. It was at the time treated as a separate diagnosis from autism, and alongside "Pervasive Developmental Disorder—Not Otherwise Specified." The distinctions were often fuzzy, and related to whether certain types of other delays or additional behaviors were present, as well as how high-functioning the patient seemed to be. Recently in the The Diagnostic and Statistical Manual of Mental Disorders (DSM-5), the latest edition of the diagnostic manual, the three separate diagnoses have been organized into one—"Autism Spectrum Disorder (ASD)"—based on our current understanding of the disorder and how it can present.

Discovering that there was a real problem in my way with a name and known properties brought tremendous relief. Though there is no cure for ASD, there are libraries of research on managing and treating aspects of it. From here I could begin to learn the causes and underlying aspects of my weaknesses, define my strengths, and begin to work toward gaining control. The relief alone was life changing, and while not eliminated, the burden of depression became vastly more manageable.

It has now been nearly a decade since my diagnosis, and I am in a much better place. I'm still often overwhelmed and require a lot of alone time, but I know why I need these things, and can often manage when, where, and how I get them so as to minimally impact the life I'm trying to have. I am writing this book in the hope that others who either suffer from something like this themselves, or know someone who does, can begin to understand what life may look like through the eyes of one of our group. I believe that a more general understanding of autism is the first step toward better relationships.

I've been told I have an unusual ability to explain what it's like living with autism. I hope this is true. Everyone lives with fears, and my greatest fear is the day someone else on the spectrum approaches me and says, "This isn't my experience at all! You're misleading and confusing them, and making it harder for me to get the help I need!" Unfortunately, I know this will happen eventually, because people with autism are exactly that: people. I would never make the claim that every blind person has the same personality, needs, desires, wants, life goals, or even experiences with being blind. I want to make clear that I don't intend to do so in regard to autism either. Every life is a unique experience, and what I'm trying to share here is mine: my trials, failures, challenges;

moments of despair, hope, sadness, and yes, occasional victory; and how I experienced them then, now, and possibly going forward. While I can't tell every autistic person's tale accurately, I genuinely believe that by reading mine, with my words, I can show how a life can be different, and perhaps provide ideas about how others may too be different.

CHAPTER 2
Overview:
GENERAL INSIGHTS ON AUTISM

"This book provides a comprehensive view into the life and perspective of an adult with high-functioning ASD. It provides rich information about ASD from the inside, along with many autobiographical examples that make the book very interesting to read. I think it is a "must read" for any teen/adult with ASD and their parents."

James B. Adams, Ph.D., Director of Autism/Asperger's Research Program at Arizona State University, President of Autism Society of Greater Phoenix, and parent of an adult daughter with autism

What We Perceive and Experience...

"A disability is any involuntary condition that prevents a person from being able to pursue the life they wish to live." —**Paul Louden**.

When you've just been told that someone you know and care about has been diagnosed with autism, your first question is likely, "What is autism?" Autism is a developmental disability. Understanding autism and what it looks like can make a world of difference in helping your life and theirs run more smoothly.

The description of autism can seem vague, as the diagnosis is based entirely on symptoms that can vary significantly from person to person. Doctors recognize certain patterns in behaviors and actions, and use that to aid in diagnosis. There is no blood test or brain scan we can currently use available to diagnose autism before symptoms appear. As autism is a developmental disorder, it impacts the brain and the entire life outcome. Some of the most visible symptoms involve our social delays. Those of us with autism don't usually interact in social settings in usually expected ways. We may not perceive or value facial expressions, tone of voice, or other cues that may be considered normal. As this filters all of our experiences as we grow, it not only affects who we are, but also who we will become.

The world can often seem overwhelming to us, and social interactions in particular may seem too challenging. We may avoid them, and some on the spectrum may not even develop basic social skills as a result. Often those on the spectrum find comfort in more stable and predictable situations, which can sometimes be expressed in repetitive behaviors. Other times, actions like arm flapping, noisemaking, and similar behaviors can be used to express emotions like happiness or anxiety that someone on the spectrum may not know how to comfortably interpret, manage, or share.

One thing to keep in mind as we talk about autism is that these behaviors are a symptom of a brain that not only thinks differently, but has physically developed differently. The average brain, or "neurotypical" brain (a term coming into use for those not diagnosed with mental conditions), reacts substantially differently than the autistic brain. MRI scans show significantly different brain activity in those on the spectrum than those who aren't. While this isn't yet a useful diagnostic tool, it does serve to show autism as a physical condition, and not something simply "in the mind" and just a matter of behavior. Many think of autism as a behavioral disorder, or simply a different personality type, but research and evidence show it to be more significant than that. The brain of a person with autism simply develops differently.

These differences have a variety of impacts, but a common one is difficulty with communication. We often find parts of communication challenging that are easy for those without autism. In particular, this often relates to ambiguity. Phrases like "please get me about six boxes" might seem fine, or only a little unclear, but for a person on the spectrum they might provoke severe anxiety. "Do they want five or seven? If they wanted exactly six, why didn't they say it? Will they get mad if I bring back the wrong number?" A person on the spectrum can freeze, unable to mentally work their way through, when presented with a task that someone else might consider trivial. This common focus on precision has led to high-functioning children with autism often being called "little lawyers" as they seek clarity and precision in their lives through precise language and definitions. Meanwhile, the combination of a focus on literal meaning and a corresponding lack of attention to emotional or nonverbal cues (such as tone of voice or body language) can often lead people to see those on the spectrum as cold or disconnected.

The executive function of the brain, which handles time management, motivation, and processing the general events of a day, is also affected. When this is functioning poorly, a person may have severe difficulty with motivation, even with things they enjoy. They may have difficulty staying aware of what time it is and how long they have to accomplish certain tasks. Routine tasks such as grooming, house cleaning, and mowing the lawn may lose their importance in daily living.

Another piece of the puzzle is episodic memory, or remembering the emotional value of things that happen in your life. The typical experience is to remember things as a truly personal experience: calling up a memory and connecting yourself to the emotional state at the time, sometimes being able to go as far as to experience the emotions you felt as if they were fresh.

For those of us on the autism spectrum, it's often very difficult to connect to the emotional experience of these past memories. They may not form fully, may be remembered as if they had happened to someone else, or may be remembered with severely decreased emotional attachment. Emotional memories provide motivation by reminding you how bad it feels to fail and how good it feels to succeed, they teach by experience in creating positive and negative feedback even before you take an action. This doesn't happen for me.

This whole process of remembering, projecting, and predicting emotional states and being able to understand the emotional consequences of actions is fundamental to most peoples' daily lives. People on the autism spectrum have emotional reactions to events around them, but they understand these reactions in such a different way than what is considered normal that it often appears we don't care. Often though, we just have a different way of experiencing and expressing events, and very different memories of it.

When I was young, I spent a number of years living overseas in Muslim countries, and learned about the many differences in cultures across them. Living with autism is similar to living in a different culture. We have our own ways of seeing the world.

We often do not learn from observing people around us the way a typical person does, as part of autism is a difficulty picking up on those things as well as an inability to form that social connection. As a result, we don't focus on the same things normal people focus on. A typical example might be that we don't make eye contact easily. This is because eyes are not as important to us as the mouth or other parts of the face when someone is speaking, even though a person typically gains a lot of information from the eyes.

When you have different tools for experiencing and interpreting the world, this can lead to unexpected and surprising problems. For example, a parent might say, "The trash is getting pretty full." For the parent, a large part of this communication is the emotional load—the suggestion of disapproval that it's full, the implied idea that something should be done about it, and a hint of urgency because it's being spoken aloud and action should take place soon. On the other hand, the person on the spectrum may explicitly notice that they did not include in the statement "And I'd like you to take it out" or "It's making me unhappy," and assume that because they could have said these things and didn't, they must not be trying to communicate these ideas.

For each person, these thought processes are natural and normal, but if they get into an argument about it, both will feel the other is being unreasonable when both have a valid point. Had they been communicating with someone who used the same methods for experiencing the world, the problem wouldn't have happened. The parent sees a rebellious child, who's making excuses and being pedantic, and the child sees a parent who is upset with them and they don't understand why. Nobody is happy. While it's impossible to be perfectly aware of someone else's thought processes, until you are aware they can be different, you cannot make any progress.

 ## It's a "Spectrum"—What Does That Mean?

What is the "spectrum"? This is a term that's frequently used to describe the way people tend to see autism's range of severity, but there is also a broad range of different symptoms that vary from person to person on the spectrum. Some of them are easily apparent and some are not apparent at all on the surface, but very much present in the ways we think and perceive. In summary, the symptoms and their severity cover a wide range. For example, some on the spectrum are extremely uncomfortable with personal space violation, whereas another person may have no conflict with personal space at all and can hold conversations with someone comfortably close. Others, like me, are able to hide our symptoms for short periods of time so it's not readily noticeable. Since receiving a diagnosis, my understanding has progressed and now I monitor my actions and reactions. On the opposite end of the spectrum, there are those so severely afflicted they cannot take care of themselves in daily life. Here is an important point: The diagnosis for autism is much more limited than the external symptoms you see. Autism creates many different symptoms that are coping mechanisms and can vary from person to person.

People tend to think of these symptoms as being disorders in and of themselves, but it is important that the range of symptoms be looked at generally as a series of coping mechanisms. Those are the ways we have learned to deal with a world of information that is coming in and can be otherwise unmanageable for us. There's a difference between what you see and what autism is inside us. Autism is a mental disability, something that happens inside the mind and brain, and there's simply no way for you to see that and fully understand it. It changes how those of us on the spectrum experience the world. As an example, someone on the spectrum may rock back and forth. Rather than a defining symptom of autism, this is likely a coping mechanism to block out an overload of incoming stimulus.

Imagine your child was born with eyes uniquely damaged in a way that was like looking through a slightly green-tinted lens, so it would be as if she were wearing faintly green-tinted sunglasses but no one knew. It would just shift the colors she saw only a little bit. Very often she could identify and recognize the differences of colors, but there would be some instances that challenged her as if she were presented with a light green paper and a white paper beside it. In that case, the colors might appear to be the exact same to the child, but to you, the white paper would be much different.

That's basically what autism is, a way of shifting information that comes into the mind. It's not just like being a different color, but it causes me to have a different way of interpreting the information. If you see a child is wearing green glasses, then you can help him understand he's not seeing his colors like everyone else and may get them wrong. But if the child is born with green-tinted lenses, an invisible difference to the outside individual, you may get into arguments and disagreements with her because you don't understand why she doesn't seem to able to tell two things apart that are obviously different. You might think she is being stubborn or rebellious or sarcastic. By understanding what is happening with autism, it helps all of us find ways to approach or work around situations.

When something causes stress, we all try to find ways to relieve it. Extreme stress is a significant symptom for those of us on the spectrum. Attempts at stress reduction are often manifested as arm slapping, spinning, or various unusual behaviors in those more significantly affected by autism. Others on the spectrum may retreat to video games, which are a world of lower stress owing to their clear rules and outcomes.

However, if I don't exhibit these or other different behaviors, that doesn't necessarily mean I'm doing fine. Even if I have coping mechanisms that cause me to appear normal and I don't have sudden outbursts that might be expected of someone on the spectrum, it still takes a lot of energy because it's an active process. I have to be engaged in many areas where those without autism can passively participate and use what comes naturally as a way of interacting with people. I'm not always able to hold a lengthy conversation or interact with others for long periods of time. I tend to look more like an introvert when I need time alone to recover the tremendous amount of energy I used being around others. It always happens, but because it's a mental thing, it's invisible to others, which might make it more difficult for them to understand the seriousness of my needing time away to recover.

I have one more analogy to help you understand what it's like. I have studied and worked to get a little bit of an understanding of facial expressions, body language, tone of voice and eye contact, but it takes a conscious effort for me. Let's say you have a little bit of understanding of German, French, Portuguese, and Italian, and you are put into a room with four other people. One is speaking German, a second is speaking French, a third Portuguese, and the fourth Italian. They are all speaking to you at the same time, with excitement and passion and eager to hear your thoughts on what they are saying. You are doing your best to follow, but your limited understanding of their language is making it very difficult. After an extended period of this interaction, would you be fatigued? Would you just want to be alone to recover from the intensity and the stress of the encounter? I feel this way a lot as I am trying to hear your words but also consciously read and interpret your facial expressions, body language, tone of voice, and eye contact.

Mom's Story

When Paul was about five or six years old and we were around other mothers, I noticed that Paul and I did not connect the same way as other moms did with their children. Sometimes I felt like I was an inadequate mother, maybe not showing enough love or attention to Paul. Other times I felt that we had a better connection as he was not clinging or checking with me before doing things. Most people were impressed with how independent and smart he was. He always wanted to know why and I always tried to explain.

We are sometimes asked, "How could you not know your child had autism?" From the very beginning we knew he was different from other children, but being our first child, we just thought he was bright and inquisitive. As he grew older and was in Mother's Day Out and preschool, we could see more of a difference but again were often told how bright and smart he was. At home, he had some oddities that I would notice, but when I read parenting books those oddities sometimes occurred in the first born or very bright children. Rick's company transferred us a lot so we moved a number of times. Paul began to have more issues, such as not knowing names of classmates, upset stomach, forgetting assignments, and not wanting to be with the family. I read more books, took parenting classes, and talked to pediatricians, all of which told me this could be typical with the frequent moves.

We did get Paul tested three times while in school. All these tests showed he had a very high IQ, so now according to the doctors, he was bored. Reading books and more parenting classes gave me the idea of rewards. We created charts with rewards at the end of the week if certain things were done each day and marked off. As he got older, we moved up to contracts between Paul and us, and between Paul and his teachers. All of these would work for a time, but Rick and I never understood why we had to continue these to make Paul cooperate. We knew a child Paul's *age shouldn't need this type of reward system. I continued to read and research, and in high school we had Paul tested several times and sent him to therapists. At various times we were told he had anxiety disorder, ADD, and depression. We all knew something was not right and tried to figure it out. Autism was never mentioned.*

When We Need a Break — We REALLY Need It

A big challenge is learning limits, and I've gotten a good feel for where my stress level is at any given time. Now I can tell people when I'm getting too tired to spend any more time with them and that I need to go home; or tell them, "I'm sorry, but I really need to ask you guys to head on out." I have an awareness of my stress that's taken a long time for me to develop. A lot of people on the spectrum don't really have any awareness of how stressed they are, how to recover, or how long it's going to take to recover, which presents a challenge for higher-functioning individuals with autism. It's learning to recognize that self-awareness of "What stresses me, how stressed am I, and how do I recover from it?" It is an important step in figuring out how to comfortably live.

When those of us on the spectrum find ourselves in a social situation where it seems everything is going wrong, we feel like we're falling behind. Once that starts to happen, it becomes very hard to resolve things and every situation becomes more stressful, especially when there's not enough time to recover between events. It gets incrementally worse until something goes horribly wrong. Maybe we're shouting at someone or locking ourselves in a room because we don't feel like we're able to come out for a while. I've been there.

In the past, when I was not really aware of what I needed to do to recover, I could find myself in a downward spiral. I'd be in over my head and not know how to repair the damage. If you are on the spectrum, often times you can't work out how to repair the situation, and those around me usually didn't recognize what was going on until it was too late. It can be very challenging.

Of course, it is helpful for parents, teachers, and friends to learn to recognize when this is happening. Don't forget that the person on the spectrum does not think the way you would expect a person to think, as they interpret the world differently. The key is to pay attention to how someone on the spectrum reacts to what you do. Are they really being helped by what you're doing or is it just making things worse? Also, be aware that just because it doesn't appear to be helping doesn't mean that it isn't appreciated. If we are getting worse, don't be offended and don't tell us we don't appreciate your help and efforts. It is important to not take it personally no matter what happens—we have a disorder, and it's not easy. Taking the challenges we have and our reactions personally just makes it worse for everyone.

If you don't feel what you're doing is helping us, taking a step back may actually be the right choice. Giving those of us on the spectrum space or putting us in a situation where we feel we're still in control of what's going on can be very helpful. Much of what builds a person's stress is the feeling of not being in control. Things can accumulate to the point that someone trying to help causes more stress because we realize we're making others stressed. It builds up, so having the space to be left alone until we're ready to join in again can, at times, be the best option.

There is No Gray — It's Black or It's White

Another part of Autism Spectrum Disorder is black-and-white thinking. Our view of self and the world tends to be very concrete, and we rarely see the abstract. This creates a tendency toward perfectionism as well. Even tiny mistakes or the smallest imperfections can feel like monumental failures, creating high levels of anxiety on this all-or-nothing scale. You might say, "Just don't think like that; life isn't all or nothing." We would if we could.

Black-and-white thinking also applies to the trust we give others. Until recent years, I assumed that those I felt I could trust were going to be completely honest with me. I didn't recognize that things can be subtly inaccurate but not necessarily intentional. I believed if I trusted someone, I could believe everything they said just the way they said it. Alternatively, if I didn't think they were trustworthy I wanted nothing to do with them at all. The lack of gray when you're on the spectrum means we can have difficulty dealing with or understanding that not everything is necessarily absolute.

Even today, I still tend to work in absolutes, but I know there is gray, so I break things down into very small pieces that are individually black and white but still have very defined lines. As an example, think of a gray picture on a computer that's made of a bunch of little dots. If you zoom in close enough you can see many individual black dots and many individual white dots, but from a distance it looks gray. That's close to how I analyze the gray areas of life in my head since I can't really see the gray the way a typical person does. I now try to break down issues small enough to where I see the small parts of the issue that are black and white. When I put together all the smaller parts of the issue that are clearly black and white, I can see the bigger issue in a way that is close to how typical people view the gray areas of life.

I might ask myself, "Can I trust a certain person in general?" For example, if I know a person is often wrong about history, I won't trust them on history, but if they know a lot about physics, I will trust them when they talk about physics. Previously when a person would tell me something incorrect about history, I would put them in the "completely untrustworthy" group and took it personally. Now, I've learned that these mistakes on their part are not personal, and I can be accepting of them and their trustworthiness on physics. That may sound odd to you, but that's the only way I have learned to be accepting of people who aren't always correct about everything, given my mind's tendency toward black-and-white absolutes.

Mom's Story

Rick and I have learned that our words and our commitments are like a legal contract to Paul as well as an important expression of love and caring. It is his love language if you will. A couple of years ago, Paul traveled to Phoenix once a month to cohost a radio show. He would leave home on Sunday and return on Wednesday, and I would drop him off at the airport and pick him up. Paul drives, but we found that it reduced his stress and anxiety of the trip for me to do this.

One week before an upcoming trip, I found out my father needed surgery and felt I needed to be with him, which meant I wouldn't be home to pick up Paul from the airport upon his return, and Rick wasn't available. I called Paul and asked if he wanted to drive himself or wanted his sister-in-law to pick him up, and he became very upset. "Tell me the details of the surgery, why is it so important for you to be there, why are you telling me you are breaking your commitment to me instead of asking?" I did my best to explain my actions and good intentions but it didn't satisfy Paul, he became only more upset.

After much discussion with both Rick and me, Paul explained that although he tries hard to understand our position, deep within him he views our commitment very much like we view a written contract. We should live up to it regardless of circumstances unless the other party to the contract gives permission to break the arrangement.

This was a clear example that Paul isn't able to weigh priorities in an easy and natural subconscious way. Words are commitments to a person on the spectrum and should never be broken in their view. They are unable to understand or judge the relative importance of life events like getting picked up from the airport versus being there for your father's important surgery. They become angry and upset that we have not lived up to a commitment, that in their view, we easily could have. Paul also sees instances like this as indications we don't care about him and he is not important to us since we arbitrarily changed plans for reasons he couldn't understand.

In retrospect, I knew for several weeks that my dad might have surgery, and I didn't tell Paul because I wasn't sure it was even going to happen. If I had mentioned the possibility and the fact that I might need to go, he would have been prepared for my change of plans. I'm sure he still would have had to process the change of schedule, but wouldn't have felt abandoned like he did.

Dad's Story

Before we knew Paul had autism, one of the issues causing conflict was that he took conversations literally. I never realized how often our conversations involve implying what we want or assuming the other person is thinking like we are.

One example was when Paul was about fourteen. He was upstairs in the den playing video games. I called up the stairs, "Paul, we just got back from the nursery with some trees and plants and need some help unloading the truck." "Okay," Paul called back. A few minutes passed as I waited at the truck with Debbie.

Debbie gave me a look that said, "This is not going to go well." After a few more minutes, I became slightly irritated and climbed the stairs to find Paul continuing to play video games. "Are you going to come help us unload the truck?" Paul fires back, "I'm playing a video game!" I responded, "I see that, but we need help unloading the truck." Paul, again, said, "Okay."

I went back downstairs and waited with Debbie again, but Paul didn't show up. Now I was getting angry and yelled up the stairs, "Paul, come down here right now and help us unload the truck." Paul came down and said, "You should ask me nicely, and by the way, I'm right in the middle of a video game." Paul helped out but was in a very grumpy mood, as was I.

If I had known what I know today, I would have told Paul the timing I expected as well as the chore—"Come unload the truck now"—because he would not have inferred "now" as I would normally expect. Also, I would have told him why we needed to unload the truck now and why we needed his help.

CHAPTER 3
FLEXIBILITY

"Behind the Locked Door provides an autobiographical filter as seen through the lens of Paul Louden, an accomplished thinker and writer. A quick read, you will find yourself connecting the dots through his mirror, sometimes side-by-side, and sometimes over his shoulder."

Rachelle K. Sheely PhD, President, RDIconnect, Inc.

Rules are Rules

When I was younger and living at home prior to my diagnosis, we had a yard work schedule for my dad, my younger brother, and me. I became very upset one particular weekend when my brother was allowed to get out of his assigned task because of another obligation. Since he knew in advance he was supposed to be doing his part of the yard work that weekend, I believed it was his fault for not doing it. I was so furious I ended up punching a stool and unintentionally breaking my hand. I didn't understand why allowances could be made for anything that wasn't an emergency. In my mind he had a schedule, and he should have done his chore before the other obligation.

I also got really frustrated with the idea of my dad being the authority. Our schedule allowed for the three jobs we had to do each week that included mowing, trimming, and edging the yard. Each week the three of us rotated the jobs, and it always frustrated me that my dad was on the schedule but seemed to have the right to say, "Well, I'm not doing it this week because I have to…" I was irritated because I couldn't understand why he put his name on the schedule if he might not do his assigned task every time.

I got to the point that I asked him to sign the schedule, and then when he still couldn't be there, I got so frustrated I didn't even know how to express it. I just didn't understand the concept of parental authority. In my mind, an agreement between two people is an agreement, and it does not matter what your position is relative to each other. Once the agreement is made, you have to stick to it. He could use his position beforehand to alter the agreement because he's the dad, but once he put himself on the schedule, he had a commitment to me. I had no authority to punish him for not upholding his part the way he could punish me, and I just couldn't understand how that was permissible. It was a big hurdle for me.

Later in college, I had the same difficulties. It drove me nuts that an instructor could be five or ten minutes late, but if I arrived late I was penalized. The anxiety built up to the point that I didn't want to go to class at all if the professor would arrive five or ten minutes late. I didn't know how to deal with it, I needed the concreteness. If I'm told a class starts at 10 A.M., the professor needs to be there at that time. Otherwise, I have an anxiety attack because I can't be late but they can. This kind of behavior probably frustrates a typical person as well, but for someone on the spectrum who lacks an inherent flexibility, the pressure builds and builds until there's some sort of breakdown.

Another issue I've had is with authority figures saying "Next time do it better" or "Do it this way because that's what I want." This is a recipe for disaster. We need to understand the why and how more than others. Take it slow, be as specific as you can, and then try confirming if we understand your expectations. Even though we can hold conversations, laugh at jokes, and even appreciate the same TV shows, please don't assume all is coming easily. It's assumed if I can figure out these things, I should be capable of figuring out the rules of life. But that's not always the case. That's autism, and we can't explain to you why.

 ## Gray = Anxiety

Anxiety hovers over a person on the spectrum like a gray cloud. The world is very stressful because uncertainty looms everywhere. This is why I prefer to do things I can control, like playing video games or computer programming. These activities have rules and are structured in a way that rules can't be broken. If I play a board game, rules can be interpretative or even modified sometimes, while video games give me a controlled and predictable environment. That's also why I like passive entertainment like books and movies.

What do you want for dinner tonight? If the average person is asked that, usually a meal idea will quickly just pop into their heads. Believe it or not, preparing meals or deciding what to eat can be filled with stress for someone on the spectrum. I have a mental process I use now so I don't panic at the question of what to eat, but it took a while to get here. I have a short list of foods

I know I like to eat, think what I've eaten this past week, and choose something from my list that I haven't had. For some, living with a parent or partner who decides what to prepare for dinner every evening can be comforting. It takes one more weight off the shoulders that many don't know exists.

Improvement comes only as I work on it. Intellectually I know what causes me stress, and as hard as I try when things don't go as planned, it remains difficult to handle. I wish I could tell you why but I don't have the answer yet. I continue to work on flexibility and I've gotten to a degree of understanding. I might have a dinner planned with my dad at 6 p.m., and at 6:05 he alerts me via text that he just left his office and is running late. It is extremely frustrating, as I realize I could have known before I left home but wasn't aware until it was too late. Driving even a short way requires a great deal of focus for me, so leaving and coming back is not a good option. I wait, but it can become so frustrating that I find myself in tears. I've gotten better at hiding my anxiety, but it is extremely difficult for me when someone is late.

I have gotten better at putting frustration and anxiety aside when it's out of my control, but when someone voluntarily breaks an agreement, or doesn't bother to let me know ahead of time, I have a hard time managing. A typical person has some flexibility a person on the spectrum doesn't, nor do we have a way to release the stress that builds inside. There's no tool for unwinding after the fact or just letting it go. Unfortunately, the lesson often learned for me is "Don't trust this person anymore." It ties back to my dependence on absolutes, and I learn lessons differently because I see the world through my filter.

I'm sure most people have a sliding scale for damage done by broken trust, a cultural ideal learned from those in their sphere of influence. For example, if your significant other cheats on you, that's a serious violation. If they show up late for a dinner date, that's a minor issue. Intellectually I understand the difference, but I still see it as a deal breaker. If a person tells me they are going to do something at a certain time and they don't, it breaks my trust. If they betray my confidence, it's broken trust.

Dad's Story

Lack of flexibility is a huge challenge for Paul. When he was young, it caused many challenges. The most basic errand like running to the grocery store for a few quick items could turn into a big issue.

One Super Bowl Sunday, Debbie, Paul, our other son Brian, and I headed to the grocery store before the game to pick up snacks. We went to the express "Eleven items or less" line, arriving just in front of two women with an assortment of groceries. Ahead of us was a big guy with a number of items. Without thinking, Debbie and I inventoried both baskets and felt a sudden stress. Both the women behind us and the guy in front of us had more than eleven items. I quickly stopped my conversation with Brian and tried to get Paul's attention. "Paul, what video game is that you are playing on your Game Boy?"

Unfortunately, it was too late. Paul's voice seemed louder and clearer than the grocery store intercom. "That man has fourteen items, not eleven." The big man looked back at Paul and me with a condescending and slightly irritated look as I said, "The six packs count as one item because they have one price, so it's okay," while preparing for the debate that was surely coming. Meanwhile, Brian looked hurt that I had left my conversation with him so abruptly. Paul said, "In that case, there are thirteen items," to which I responded, "It's fine, thirteen is close to eleven and the checkout lines are packed." The burly man was clearly irritated now while Debbie tried to step in position to prevent Paul from counting the items in the basket behind us, which clearly had over eleven items as well. "It doesn't say thirteen, it says eleven and they have more than eleven too!" Paul shouted. Brian slid into the background, intensely studying the magazines for sale. Debbie turned to the lady behind us, "I've been meaning to try that wine," as she tried to be polite and divert attention from Paul's comments. And so it went, just a quick trip to the grocery before the Super Bowl.

CHAPTER 4

APPEARANCE AND HYGIENE

"Paul does a tremendous job providing a firsthand account of how he perceives the world and how that perception has affected his relationships with everyone in his life. For educators, his description of how he struggled to manage school, all the way through high school, illuminates how the world of a child with ASD differs from the "neuro-typical" child."

Anne Donahoo, M.Ed., NCC, NCSC, Director of Counseling Services & Upper School Counselor, The John Cooper School

When it comes to the issues of appearance and hygiene, people on the autism spectrum tend to think very differently than the average person. We may not understand how or why our hygiene affects the people around us. Though typical people are aware of the social stigma of being with someone whose clothes are soiled or may smell a certain way, we don't necessarily understand or relate to social stigmas and don't notice someone else's discomfort. We may not even notice that we look unkempt or different from people around us, as that is not something we are always aware of.

I view hygiene as mostly a cultural issue, something that became important to people just a few hundred years ago. Some remote cultures still don't worry much about hygiene, and modern cultures across the globe have views of proper hygiene that frequently differ from one another. If you are trying to explain to someone on the spectrum they should get in the habit of doing something every day for hygiene purposes, it may not register well as it may appear to be an unnecessary hassle requiring the self-motivation and self-management that we find very difficult.

Not everyone on the spectrum has hygiene issues, but it is very common. Those issues may vary from person to person, so while some might not shower as often, others have larger issues with dental hygiene. You may explain why we need good hygiene, but if it is not explained in a way we can understand or relate to, we may not agree on its importance. I don't believe there is a simple solution for hygiene with people on the spectrum; you will have to patiently work with them to find the best solution for that individual person.

As a personal example, I don't mind taking showers, it doesn't cause any issues for me, but I still have a difficult time doing it. I like the water fine, but it still absolutely stresses me to take one every day on a regular schedule. As some days I don't leave the house, what works for me is to skip showers if I'm staying home and take a shower before I leave the house so I am acceptable to the people who will be around me. I'm still not motivated to take a shower "for me," but have decided to do it for these social reasons.

For those on the spectrum, one of the most important parts of life is figuring out what parts of their schedule are most stressful for them. In terms of showering, is it the ritual or the actual cleaning, the water or the strict scheduling, or maybe it's the shampoo? Finding the right solutions and compromises is not easy but can help solve the problem. As a parent, think about the issue of hygiene as a huge challenge and consider how their mind is wired as opposed to thinking, "My child just doesn't like to take a bath and it is such a hassle" or "My child is being disobedient by not doing what I say."

Remember that motivation, self-control, and self-discipline can be extremely difficult for those of us on the spectrum. Even some things I really enjoy and like to do, I still have difficulty doing on a regular basis. For reasons I can't explain, I don't have that internal motivating force that I see in other people. Even as an adult, I sometimes need to rely on my mom or family to keep me on track. This is not necessarily the case with everyone on the spectrum, but even though I'm considered "high functioning," I am willing to say I need help in some areas and if I know someone is there who is not judging me, that helps a lot.

Dad's Story

Even as a young adult in his late teens and early twenties, Paul still had trouble motivating himself in some areas. He often missed brushing his teeth and for a period of seven to eight years he never made it to the dentist. Eventually he went, and his teeth were in very bad shape. Ultimately he had to have many of his teeth extracted and implants installed. A huge challenge for parents of young adults on the spectrum is we no longer have control to ensure our children take care of themselves or make appropriate decisions, but they often still need our help.

CHAPTER 5

EPISODIC MEMORY

"We tend to expect those around us to think the same way; this book is a good reminder that people with autism may have a very different way of expressing emotions. A short, insightful read for parents and teachers of people with autism spectrum disorder. The author, who has ASD, uses examples from his own life to explain some of the thinking processes that may be different in autism. The brief vignettes from the points-of-view of family members round out the examples and are very helpful, so the reader can see the issues from both the neuro-typical and the autistic perspectives."

Gary W. Moore, Co-Founder & President, nonPareil Institute

Memory of Emotions

How would you feel if you couldn't remember what you did for your birthday last year or where you spent the holidays? Memories like that just aren't there for me. One of the hardest things I experience is my inability to remember people, events, or simple daily tasks. This is because most memories have an emotional attachment that creates a link to the memory. I have no emotional anchor linked to my memories, so my memories are like watching a movie about someone else's life. I'm very unlikely to remember things like birthdays or special occasions as a result, and even routine chores may require continual reminders.

For those of us on the spectrum, memories of the things we do fade very quickly. Without these linked emotional attachments, memory is much weaker. What most people ordinarily remember are times connected to significant events or habits that you deal with frequently. For those of us on the spectrum, there may be little to no recall of past events, things done, or words spoken. Though the memory can be reconstructed, these memories are weak and short at best. As I mentioned previously, when I was a child I found myself unable to recall having fun at the playground. It isn't that I'm not trying; I just can't recall what is gone.

Emotional memory is also known as episodic memory. Dealing with the lack of memory can be very frustrating for the parent or teacher as well as the person who can't remember. Slow improvement can happen for some with the help of different tools that provide reminders. I now record more reminders on my phone, using timers or messages, to do certain tasks. Even with that help, all of the details of a memory do not come back. A schedule with a process or plan and a regular daily routine helps those of us on the spectrum.

Having difficulty with memory or recall can cause conflicts. Forgetting to do simple chores at home can cause conflict, and long-term projects at work or school can be difficult. Projects that are given only a completion date and no plan for steps to be completed along the way are especially challenging. Breaking down the task by giving assignments in three to five day increments instead of leaving it up to the student or employee can help the person meet a goal. Without help like this, they may not even begin. This focus on one step at a time, as well as a focus on the time management involved, can be a great help.

Big projects are a challenge to most students and especially to someone on the spectrum who may visualize the project as very scary. This was a challenge for me in high school, but I benefited from reminders and a regular schedule. When this structure was absent in college, my struggles increased. Having a plan to follow and someone to follow up with you is the difference between success and failure, and it can keep someone from giving up. Self-management without memory is a difficult challenge for someone on the spectrum, so having someone who will be a coach and help keep you accountable is a valuable asset. You have to allow for flexibility, but having a plan that includes small steps can get you to your destination.

One thing that helped me in school and provided tools for other aspects of my life was studying how to program computers. Programming requires very clear steps and putting information in the correct order so that what you want is achieved at the other end. That helped me start understanding other things by breaking them down into small pieces, into shades of gray.

 ## Emotions — Do We Have Them?

This is a topic I'm asked about a lot. The answer is yes, we do have emotions just like you, but we are not affected by those emotions the same way, don't express them the same, and don't remember or recall them very well. I find that people often make assumptions based on what they see and hear from a person on the spectrum. When I'm observed acting in a typical way, others assume I'm capable of doing all the mental gymnastics they do, but it goes even beyond that. There are ways typical people think that are so fundamental that it's simply called "human nature" and is not even questioned. Even when you see someone with various mental challenges, you still think that the underlying human nature is the same for everyone and that this person with challenges just does things differently.

Autism is like having a different underlying nature. Typical people are very much aware of their feelings because of their emotional memories, and these understandings are readily available without much thought. Those of us on the spectrum do not have this to pull from in our encounters with others. For example, if a parent told their neurotypical child, "If you don't take out the trash, you won't be allowed to go to the swimming pool," then the child remembers how much fun he has at the swimming pool so he is motivated to take out the trash. He doesn't even need to try to recall these memories and acquire motivation from the emotional connection. You can see why this type of strategy with someone on the spectrum doesn't work very well. We don't remember the fun we had at the swimming pool, and no one hates this more than we do.

This lack of emotional memory and expression is hard for some to believe, but we really are wired this way. It's impossible for others to imagine what it's like just the same as I can't imagine what it's like to be neurotypical. It's difficult to get someone to understand—even someone who knows about our condition. They so often want to take our lack of emotional memory or lack of signs of emotion personally and I don't understand why. I feel it's very important that both sides of the spectrum be educated, especially on the neurotypical side, because frequently people on the autism spectrum are not at the point that they can be self-aware.

We see things as they are and take them at face value. Our communication is usually without the emotion others recognize and we don't know intuitively that our responses can elicit emotions in others. At Christmastime, an autistic child may inform his grandparent, "Oh, I already have this game at home," instead of politely receiving the gift. Simply making a statement, the autistic child is very straightforward with no concept of the effect on the other person.

Typical people express their emotions through subtle cues like body language and tone of voice. Those of us on the autism spectrum don't pick up on that very well. Unfortunately, people sometimes assume that we're not interested in how they feel or that we're impassive. For the higher functioning autistic individual, we tend not to express our emotions in a way that people recognize. We can be considered cold or dispassionate, even robot-like without visible emotion. This is a big misconception. We do have strong emotions going on inside, but we don't know how to recognize them in ourselves or how to express or explain them to others. Personally, mine seem disconnected because they're one step away from what's directly going on. I feel as if I'm aware of them if I look inside and search for them, but they are less of a driving force for me than most people. I can't think about my emotions and talk to someone at the same time. Don't ask me why, I just can't.

Before my diagnosis I saw others as far more passionate than me. I watched people's emotions on television, in movies, and in real life and saw how others are driven by their emotions when they are fearful, extremely angry, or jubilant. I saw how their body language changed with those emotions, and became convinced I had no internal emotional connection. Without my diagnosis, I had no one to help me figure out how to look sad or happy and listen to my own emotional responses. The responses are there, they just don't affect me the same way.

In school, my lack of showing emotion got me into trouble. I had teachers furious with me because they expected me to show remorse and feelings of regret. I would say, "I know I did something wrong, so what more do you want from me? I told you I was wrong." I wasn't showing the signs of feeling bad about it they expected, plus my body language and tone of voice were inadequate.

I had a girl break up with me. She was extremely upset because she thought I wasn't sad about it but I just wasn't showing I was upset. I was trying to intellectually control my emotions and I felt horrible, but not in the way that a typical person expresses that. She thought I was just pretending to be sad because she felt my body language and tone of voice weren't fitting the situation correctly.

Here's an interesting point: emotional understanding and expression is a very cultural thing. Japan, for example, places the emphasis on NOT expressing emotions. Regardless of where someone lives, if they are on the spectrum they will undoubtedly have the same struggle within their culture.

Let's look at another emotion: love. I think I love my parents, but no one has ever been able to tell me what "love" is or what it feels like in a way I can identify with or in a way I can say, "Oh, I can imagine that." I have emotions for my parents because I know they are pretty much one of those few things you are definitely supposed to love in your life. I think this must be what love is and sort of use it to judge other cases. I've consciously used the example of love for my parents and my brother as the measure of love that's allowed for others.

Here's what I hope you'll take away from this: autism is different on an underlying level. Instead of thinking about how a person on the spectrum communicates so differently, think about why the person communicates the way they do. It's the "why" that makes the real difference.

Mom's Story

Paul at the Playground

When Paul was close to three years old, we lived down the street from a playground. It was a beautiful day so I walked down the street to let Paul play. On it was a slide and some swings. I walked him over by the swing set where Paul got in the swing by himself and started swinging. He looked around and saw all the other mothers sitting on the benches. He told me "Mom, you must go sit on the bench." After I was on the bench for a few minutes, not very long, he came over and asked, "What do I do now?" I suggested he go slide some more or swing some more. He went over and slid a few more times, swung in the swing a few more times, and returned to me. Looking at me he told me, "I have done that, now what?" I took his hand and we walked back home. I was very confused as to why he did not enjoy the playground or play with the other kids. I now know he did not get the same enjoyment of running around as the other children that day because he couldn't imagine and he didn't have memories of the pleasure of sliding and swinging.

Dad's Story

A few years ago, Paul and I took a walk around the neighborhood. There were an unusual number of homes for sale and they all had little brochures available at the curb as we walked by. In my eagerness to build rapport with my son I said, "Paul, how many square feet do you think that house is and what price do you think it's selling for? I'm going to guess 2500 square feet and a price of $250,000." Paul responded with "I don't know." His response didn't discourage me. I continued, "Just guess, it'll be fun to see how close we come." Paul obliged. "Okay, tell me this one and I'll guess the next one."

We had a great time as some we were close on and some we were far from right. We joked, kidded each other, and laughed and it felt great having a normal father and son experience. Arriving home Debbie asked, "How was your walk?" I was on a high because experiences like this with Paul were not common. "We had a blast, didn't we Paul?" Paul with no excitement in his voice responded with "I guess."

I was taken aback, "I guess?" Paul said, "I don't know if we had fun; we looked at houses and guessed size and price." I couldn't believe it. "But it was great fun; we were both laughing about our guesses and all kinds of things." Paul with a puzzled look on his face remarked, "I just remember what we did but not if we had fun, why would that be fun?"

CHAPTER 6
MOTIVATION

"Paul is so honest in telling his story, including the good with the bad. That is real life! There are no two people with autism who are just alike, but there is a common thread that runs through their lives and experiences where they can relate to each other. The more information that gets out about autism, the better the world can understand and appreciate people on the spectrum. I gained a great deal of insight from this book, but the thing that really opened my eyes was the chapter on motivation. I have tried for years to teach motivation to my student and Paul gave me such good insight as to why that is difficult."

Janice Magness, Director, Burkhart Transition Academy and Burkhart Center for Autism Education & Research

What Motivates Me...

Motivation has always been a big challenge for me. The lack of positive emotional memories limits motivation, and accomplishing anything in life ultimately requires successful interactions with others. The stress of foreseeing those interactions that don't always go right for me also limits my motivation. What motivates me most of the time is curiosity. When I'm learning something or having new ideas, I work well, but as soon as I know enough about it, like solving the interesting part of the problem or trying the new idea, my curiosity is satisfied and I have a hard time continuing. Even if it's something I intellectually know I want to do or if it's something I know I love doing, I struggle to find the motivation I need to follow through. Intellectual knowledge doesn't get people moving, it is the emotional reactions or expected emotional feeling that gets you started and those are absent in me.

I used to never understand why we would travel to visit family. Without episodic memories or emotional attachment to them, I simply wasn't motivated to go to the trouble of packing and making a trip. Christmas was pretty much the same way. Since I had no emotional memory about Christmas or the thrill of Christmas morning, I wasn't motivated to anticipate the excitement and fun. Those were depressing times for my mom because she thought she was being a bad mother and later she faced the same thing when I had difficulties in high school although I was intellectually very capable. She blamed herself when my behavior didn't fit the norm.

Since I normally have a hard time with motivation, having my family around helps significantly because they can get me started on something. Once I start a project I'm usually involved until I stop, and then it's hard to get going again. If I stop for a lunch break, three hours later it's really hard to pick up where I left off.

I have a regular schedule now where I meet my mom several times a week and we just talk about what's going on. This process of talking through it helps me keep better track and it keeps those memories and thoughts fresh, providing an impetus to stay with it. I still have strong problems with motivation, but a regular schedule mitigates some of that. Without the memory mechanism in place, you have to use other ways to motivate yourself.

I travel quite a bit, and if I didn't have someone to give me a ride to the airport, eventually I probably wouldn't go. I know that I wouldn't be able to make my own reservations regularly over the long term and that I would put it off or forget about it. Even with all that I've learned, I struggle to keep up with everything. Without the ability to put my bills on an automatic debit, I'd probably have a real challenge getting them paid every month. I've met people on the edge of the spectrum who are tremendously motivated, and I've also met many who are just as challenged with motivation as I am.

Building Up to Getting Motivated and Pacing to Stay Motivated

A big part of motivation for me in almost everything I do is having time to build up to an event, like a mental long jump. You can't do the long jump from a standing start; you need a run-up to it. I need to get a mental run-up to almost everything. Being able to visualize something in advance helps me know what I need to do to get that process moving in my mind.

Getting up in the mornings is hard for me because of my lack of motivation. Part of it is depression, which I do take medication for. People on the spectrum are much more vulnerable to depression than people in the general population. When I began living on my own, I tried going to school and then working. This life, with all the things that challenged and frustrated me, was very stressful for me. Now, because I've learned how to make enough time to recover, to keep my energy high and to rebuild it after stressful events, it's not so bad. I don't dread getting up.

There are days I eat only one meal a day because it takes me until 4 P.M. to get up the energy to prepare the food or go out and pick up something. If I'm relaxing, I really don't have much energy at all. I need a lot of recovery time between the coming and going that I have to do; it's just the way of life for me. It may be more from the depression than the autism, but that's something many people on the spectrum struggle with.

A large thing about life and staying motivated for those of us on the spectrum is pacing. We need to figure out a pace we can maintain. Not trying to push much beyond that pace can make a big difference and is best. The challenge is in finding your limits.

Watching movies or a little television has a calming effect on me. I like reading, video games, music, or anything I can do at my own pace or have control over. I listen to audio books a lot. For me, it all boils down to having time when I know someone's not going to knock on my door or walk up the stairs and ask if I can help them with something. It's time that I see as constant and won't be interrupted. It's not about what I'm doing at the time. It's that I know something isn't going to interrupt me. That downtime gets me ready for whatever happens next.

When it comes to being motivated to maintaining my daily life, I have to deal with all the stresses inherent in being on the spectrum. A lot of my stress is not inherently about the schedule I have as much as it is the commitment to someone else involved in the schedule. If I try to create a schedule for myself, I fall behind, make excuses, and end up canceling a lot of things on the list. That's what happened when I went off to college to live completely on my own. Even if the schedule is something like meeting my mom somewhere, I start making excuses because the stress of driving to meet her is big for me.

Driving is a significant stressor for me, particularly when other people don't use their turn signal or they speed. I can't explain why and it doesn't help to tell me just ignore it. Although it's stressful, once in the car and driving, I've learned to handle it. But beforehand I think, "Oh, I really don't want to go out today." That's why when I go out with my mom, most of the time I prefer she just picks me up.

I know that I will generally meet my mom for lunch twice a week on Monday and Thursday. Having someone else involved in my life, but not telling me I need to do something, makes a significant difference. Just knowing that I'll be sitting down and talking with her each week makes life more regular for me. It helps me keep track of time progressing, because when those of us on the spectrum don't have a firm schedule, we can lose track of time.

Scheduling does seem to help most people on the spectrum. The key is figuring out how to incorporate it into life in a way that doesn't increase the anxiety or depression so common with those on the spectrum. Knowing what works for the person and what doesn't is really important, but the difference from one individual to another can be hard to figure out and take some time.

What helps me the most is planning for one event at a time. It's not so much the scheduling specifically as it is having a constant reminder that something is coming up, which allows me to slowly build mental preparation for what is going to happen. Knowing what's coming for the week ahead is important. A more intense schedule like the trip I took to Bali for an RDI conference takes much longer to mentally prepare.

Knowing that something is coming far enough in advance helps me to keep it in mind and reduces any anxiety I may have. I really depend on Google Calendar on my phone and computer, which I look at frequently. It allows me to see what's happening for the next few days and it stays in my mind. Seeing an event is coming three or four days in advance makes me feel less rushed and more at ease.

Understanding My Limits — When to Temporarily Withdraw and Recharge

In addition to the observable symptoms, each of us with autism is dealing with many inward issues, such as, "How do I motivate myself? What type of social interaction can I deal with today and for how long? How long can I be out in the world before I need time to recover?" These thoughts are hard to put on a scale and quantify.

Regardless of where a person is on the spectrum, it requires a great deal of mental energy to function day to day. Some people can't recover fast enough to regularly interact with others. It depends on what we've learned, what we know, and what skills we've developed. Some on the spectrum may not recognize certain things they need to be doing and consequently are not spending energy doing them.

I used to be relatively unaware of the people around me and wasn't conscious of their emotional state, though I did spend a lot of time trying to repair things when there was a misunderstanding as a result of the way my brain processes interactions. Eventually I understood that I am supposed to be aware of what is going on with others, but I don't have the filter in place that typical people develop growing up that helps gauge the intensity of an emotional reaction and its relative importance. Now when someone else present makes a sound such as a sigh or they shift in their seat, something in my brain begins to evaluate them. Are they bored? Are they uncomfortable? Do I need to ask if they want me to do something? I have to spend a lot of energy to consciously evaluate my response. Do I need to react to this, or is it something I can ignore?

As I became more aware of what it meant to be autistic and the challenges I faced, I actually ended up spending more energy on things I hadn't before. I needed to ensure that the people around me were comfortable, and learning how much energy I can spend on that versus how much energy I need to hold back to keep myself comfortable.

The amount of energy someone on the spectrum has to spend to maintain awareness of those around us, something typical people do subconsciously, can leave us exhausted very quickly. I have to devote so much focus to monitoring tone of voice, body language, and other nonverbal communication, that I often find myself exhausted very quickly. Eventually, my patience wears thin and I can become easily frustrated. When others mumble, talk to themselves, or sigh a lot, I might ask them not to do it. "If you're not talking to me, please don't speak, because of what I have to go through to evaluate it." I might get terse with them as a result, probably won't explain myself well either, and then they will be offended.

Many people on the spectrum become stressed in social situations and don't know how to pinpoint the source. Thankfully, I have spent enough time trying to figure myself out that I realize what's happening to me. When you don't recognize what's causing the stress, you don't have the tools to ask for help in finding a way to make the situation easier. This is when withdrawal, such as locking yourself in your room, becomes the best option. Unfortunately, people around you might not understand what you're trying to do, and are at a loss for helping to resolve the situation because the required communication isn't there. Temporary withdrawal is how we cope and regroup.

To change a behavior of someone on the spectrum, there have to be ways to relieve the stress we're feeling. Forcing a change in unwanted behaviors and/or coping mechanisms isn't necessarily the answer. We need to be aware of and address the source of the stress before we can change our reactions to the situation.

CHAPTER 7
COMMUNICATION

"As a second-grade teacher, I have had multiple students on the spectrum, both diagnosed and undiagnosed, and yet I've had very little training on the best strategies to work with these students. By hearing the thoughts of an adult trying to explain his experience helped me see how a student might be experiencing the world and why my interactions do not have the effect that I think they will have. I especially found it valuable to hear about emotions, expectations and communication."

Christine Cohen, 2nd grade teacher

A Different Way of Communicating

When I lived overseas, I saw people trying to learn a new language. When you have someone fluently speaking a language to someone who is still learning, it's difficult. Someone new to the language tends to speak very literally; they don't understand the idioms, the body language, or the tone of voice that are used because they're focusing on what the words mean. Fortunately, a lot of times people learn how to handle that, and when you know the other person doesn't understand, you may slow down, or you may realize he's reacting in a way you didn't expect and think you should stop and ask for clarification. This same scenario can apply to communicating with a person on the spectrum.

When two neurotypical people interact, whether in a normal conversation or a disagreement, they are both reading each other's body language and listening to each other's tone of voice. There's an emotional flow between them. One sees the other being more agitated and may push that, unconsciously making them feel bad. He may be signaling "I'm angry and I want you to share my discomfort." Or, on the other hand, he may back off and try to make the other person feel better and attempt to lower the level of agitation.

People on the autism spectrum often focus more on literal things, so we may not even have noticed that this emotional component is taking place, or that the other person is both transmitting and trying to receive emotional data. When someone is sending emotional data to those of us on the spectrum, and from their perspective it seems we're ignoring the data, it tells them the situation is not important to us, and we don't even know we are sending that message. That may not be our intention, but we're basically holding a different conversation than they are.

In a conversation with a neurotypical person, one may get frustrated and feel "I'm getting angry and they don't even care that I'm angry, so now I'm going to get angrier." The reality is not necessarily that the autistic person doesn't care, but we don't know how you expect us to act and the reaction doesn't come naturally like it does for you. You haven't told us you're angry, or communicated to me in a way I can understand that you are angry. You may not think we're angry because we're saying, "I'm really upset with you about this," but you assume we can't really be upset if we're saying it so calmly and peacefully. It sounds like it's an issue we've come to terms with when in reality the person with autism sounds calm because we aren't using an emotional channel. When we say we're upset, what doesn't show is that I'm really, really upset, possibly even furious right now, but I'm not showing it in any way other than my words. In this situation, there are two completely different conversations going on, and we each have different tools for adding weight and importance to what we are saying.

Generally, two typical people communicate well enough to get by. There may be misunderstandings, but they're usually not big enough to make a difference because each one has the same tool kit, and if they want to work out the differences, they can. The same thing happens with people who are high-functioning on the spectrum. Frequently, we're able to communicate well with each other to a degree. It's when you have people with different enough mental processes that things start really becoming a problem.

Understanding how this communication can work takes a combined effort that involves understanding that (a.) autism is a disability, and (b.) therapy is there to help people on the autism spectrum better interact with typical people. When you talk about difficulties faced by people in wheelchairs, you know you can put in a ramp or install an elevator. You look for compromises that don't make the situation worse, but offer them an opportunity to use the skills that they do have. In dealing with autism, society doesn't yet have that compromise mentality. Hopefully, as we get a broader understanding of autism, we can better understand how to interact with one another. If people on both sides of the spectrum leverage whatever strengths they have, maybe we can work together to make it easier for everybody on both sides.

Language and Communication

Many people don't really think about what communication is and how it works, particularly language. If two people are holding a conversation and speak the same language, they usually understand each other and relate, but communication involves many more parts than most people tend to think about.

One important part of communication is body language. People don't tend to think about it, but it greatly impacts how people interpret communication from another person. There's also tone of voice, which again most people don't think about, but it factors into how people interpret things being said; things like deciding if a person is being sarcastic or insulting when they speak to us or whether they're joking at our expense.

There can be an underlying assumption that a word means the same thing to you as it does to someone else. Instead, there are situations when words are not used by their dictionary definition, but used colloquially. These different or added meanings to simple words can be very challenging to those of us who have difficulty with communication in the first place.

Since those on the autism spectrum often struggle with flexibility, we often don't have the tools in place to help when miscommunications are happening. We may not value body language or tone of voice as much, and we may miss when a word is being used in a different context.

Communication can be a real challenge for those on the spectrum and miscommunication becomes a larger struggle. Frequently, neurotypical people will either notice when a miscommunication happens or when the other person isn't acting as expected. For example, when something is meant to be a joke but the other person doesn't laugh or instead, tenses up, a typical person will recognize the miscommunication. They'll recover the situation and relationship easily by saying, "Oh, no, I didn't mean it that way." Those on the autism spectrum likely won't catch that something has gone wrong until it's so late in the interaction that it has become a real problem.

There are several different channels of communication, and to best explain myself, I've split them into four categories. The first is *explicit verbal,* which is simply the words you choose to say. That is easily taught and grasped by those on the spectrum. Next, there is *explicit nonverbal,* or body language and vocal tone, things most typical people do subconsciously or intentionally. This does not come naturally to those on the spectrum, but can be taught and learned to some extent.

Then there's *implicit nonverbal* that overlaps significantly with body language, and comes naturally for typical people. These are the parts of communication that are cultural and seem fundamental to most people. For example, a louder voice means anger if coupled with certain tone or body language, but might mean excitement or happiness if coupled with another tone or body language. On the other hand, in some cultures, being quiet means you're angry. These types of communications aren't taught and are hard for someone on the spectrum to recognize on the spot.

Last, *implicit verbal* is the assumption that everyone has the same understanding about words and language. Usually, you'll see two people talking and one will use the completely wrong word for something, but because the other person understood the general train of thought, they recognize the intended meaning and pass right by the misstep without stopping the conversation. This is another area that is never taught or thought much about. Those of us on the spectrum have trouble with this as we understand language is fluid but we can see words only as concrete.

Those of us on the spectrum tend to pick up language a lot more formally and tend to see words as a lot more concrete and structural, which can cause real difficulties, particularly in regard to our flexibility with words. As an example, in the classroom a child with autism may ask a question about an error, and he appears to be the "little lawyer" or "little professor" stereotype. The child is not really looking for errors, but struggling to understand why the words are written in a particular way. People on the autism spectrum learned language this way and don't understand how to interpret it when others are more casual in their language than those on the spectrum can understand.

A large part of helping those on the spectrum is wrapped up in the question of mental flexibility. If an issue arises when your child or anyone on the spectrum appears sarcastic, snotty, or stuck-up, think of it as a communication breakdown that must have occurred. You as the neurotypical person have the flexibility to step back and decide how to improve the situation by asking a question, such as, "Okay, you just said something that upset me. Did you intend to upset me? Or were you trying to think of a different way to tell me something?"

While the person on the autism spectrum may not have the tools to be flexible, the parent, teacher, or coworker does have the flexibility and needs to be cognizant to use those tools rather than treating the conversation like a normal one. If something seems to go awry, be flexible. Ask, "Is this what you said?" and repeat what you heard and how you understood that. Don't get upset if what they say seems offensive. The person on the spectrum may not fully grasp the meaning of what they said or the tone of voice they used. If they say no, take a step back and reassess what's going on so you can end the situation in as positive a way as possible. It's better for everyone.

Learning what a person on the spectrum really means when they talk to you can be challenging. Knowing how to respond can make things go more smoothly. When a child on the spectrum tells you something, repeat it back by saying, "Here's what I think it means, is that what you mean?" If it still seems odd, try to think of it as though she may be following a particular rule. Look at it and say to yourself, "Maybe that's not what she meant to say." You may be taking it in terms of an insult when that's really not what was intended. They may reply, "No, I mean what I said, not what you're thinking." That can come across as insulting although it's not meant to be; instead they can't grasp another way to say it.

If a parent says, "What do you think about these new shoes?" and the child says, "I don't like those shoes," that can very easily sound insulting, but it's not meant to be. The child is being honest, which is a good quality, and doesn't know how to handle that situation. The child just may be thinking she personally doesn't care for that style shoe or wouldn't wear those shoes. A common example of this situation comes at holidays or birthdays when a child or young adult receives a gift and is asked by a well-meaning grandparent, "Do you like it?" The answer given is not always the expected appropriate answer.

You have to be patient if you are going to understand what the person on the spectrum is trying to communicate. Ask questions to confirm what the person is trying to say. Personally, I often find people putting words in my mouth because they're taking significantly more meaning out of what I say than what I tried to communicate. I sometimes try to be more literal and precise, but when I do, people often feel like I'm talking down to them. It can be a very difficult position to be in for those on the spectrum when we're trying to talk and communicate effectively.

I don't understand how typical people can have this unique knack for saying things in a nonliteral way but still have confidence in what the other person is going to assume from it. There's a flow of communication that's beyond my ability to comprehend; I see it happening but I don't know how to do it.

It's often very difficult for me to talk to people without upsetting them. One of the goals of this book is to help people understand that upsetting others is not the intention of those of us on the spectrum, and that social communication is one of the key weak areas of autism. It's not that it can't be done; it just takes on a different look than the typical communication of people.

Often, I really need the help of other people to communicate better with them. When I say, "Look, I'm having a hard time knowing how to talk to you," the response I often get is "Well, you need to get better at it." It's very stressful for me when typical people tell me, the one who has been diagnosed with a weakness in this area that has a physical basis in my brain, that I'm the one who needs to make all the effort to communicate better. It's very frustrating and upsetting to have people around you refusing to use their strength and flexibility to attempt to better our communication, and leaving it all up to me. I am working on this area, but until I get to the point I'm not struggling, I would really like the help of other people to communicate better with them.

Dad's Story

Paul's Friend at the Mall

One Saturday afternoon, our family was Christmas shopping at the mall. Coming our way was another family with a little girl and a boy about Paul's age. The boy saw Paul, smiled, and said, "Hey, Paul." Debbie and I were surprised and very happy that someone was going out of their way to be friendly to our son. Paul didn't even look up and kept walking. The boy tried again with great confidence. "Paul, hey, how's it going?" Paul didn't seem to hear him, yet we all heard him loud and clear. Debbie touched Paul's shoulder and encouraged him, "This boy is saying hi to you." Paul hardly looked up and replied, "Oh." The other family now had come right up to us and the boy was still trying his best to get Paul to respond. I took ahold of Paul and said, "You need to say hi to that boy. Do you know him from school?" Debbie tried to engage the other parents in a quick conversation but it was difficult as they were slightly irritated and embarrassed that their son was being ignored. We all continued as quickly as we could to get out of this awkward situation.

Debbie explained to Paul that when someone says hello we need to respond back. Paul's face showed no sign of comprehension or acknowledgement but he said, "Okay." I couldn't understand what happened or why my son acted that way. How could he be so oblivious?

CHAPTER 8
SOCIAL
INTERACTIONS

"Paul's book gave me more insight on how the autistic brain functions and helped me to understand better some of my grandson's actions and behaviors. Since my autistic grandson is nonverbal and unable to communicate his feelings and emotions, this book really helped me to understand how stressful that must be for him every day. Thank you, Paul, for that insight!"

Jere Lynn Burkhart, grandmother and legal guardian of a nonverbal 31-year-old grandson.

Be Yourself or Fit In?

When you are a young child on the spectrum and the media is telling you to "Be yourself" and express your individuality, some things can seem confusing or overwhelming, as we still find ourselves in situations where we are being encouraged to "fit in." We should dress like other kids and act in a way others consider "normal" even though we may not understand what "normal" is. We may not even understand nonverbal cues like a smile, frown, or someone signaling us to come over. Are we supposed to "be ourselves" or "fit in"? When we get it wrong, we're different enough that it causes difficulties for other people and upsets them.

The people around us, like teachers, parents, and others, say we need to get along with everyone, which requires "fitting in," but how do we do that? TV shows and media show us a certain way the world is or should be, but when we go out day to day, we're told that reality is the exception, and things aren't like that. Even though I'm on the autism spectrum, people assume I'll figure out what I'm really supposed to do between being myself and fitting in and how to mix the two. Unfortunately, these aren't things I can really understand well and there is not a good way to help me through this.

Those of us on the spectrum use tremendous mental energy in making the effort to figure out these difficulties in interactions we experience. We don't know or understand what is expected of us. It takes a lot of energy to figure out what the expectation is and what we are doing wrong, and then to be able to recognize it when we are doing it. Often someone tells us to do something and we do our best, but it isn't quite what they wanted.

"Implied" communication is a large struggle for those on the autism spectrum. People assume their idea is being implied, but we don't always pick up that part of the communication. We often don't see things from the other person's perspective and we may not get the big picture. We need others to explain these things so we can see why we must do something a certain way, when to do it in the future, and when situations are similar. We aren't able to visualize the connections to make all of this work, and this makes social interactions often seem confusing and overwhelming.

 ## The Bucket Theory

A big challenge of socializing is the mental energy it takes out of me. I feel as if I have one bucket of energy that I can use for interacting with people. The interaction with them uses it up over time and it comes back slowly. The more time I spend with people, the more time I need to recover from it. A short visit like going to lunch with someone doesn't really take much time to recover from, but a couple of days of seeing people and doing things with them can leave me exhausted. It takes a few days to recover. If I keep going, the closer I get to the bottom of that bucket the worse I get at having positive interactions with people. I don't notice things I need to and tend to ignore the person I'm with.

When my bucket is empty, downtime is the only solution. For me, downtime is simply just time by myself, not even around people I'm comfortable with. It's time when I don't have to focus and pay attention to all the things that are challenging to me. I can relax and be comfortable, and I'm not apt to think about things or try to figure out what's going on. I can refill my bucket.

Downtime is about being completely alone for me. Even having someone who I'm not interacting with and they're just doing their own thing can cause stress. I still have to expend energy paying attention to them when they make a movement or small noise and I have to consciously figure out if they are prompting me or can be ignored. I can't turn off my reaction to them. All of this requires a great deal more conscious energy for me than the average person.

For each person on the spectrum, what takes energy and what refills the bucket can differ. Typically though, being out and inter-acting with people is challenging for anyone on the spectrum. What counts for "downtime" can be different because we have different types of alone activities that can help us recover. For some, it may even be flapping hands or making noises, which are ways of letting go of that drained feeling.

During my alone time, I have to know I will have a long enough period of time before something else is scheduled. If I'm meeting someone the next morning, it may not work as downtime because I'll be anxious about whether I'll be recovered and ready. As long as I have that anxiety, I won't be calming down and fully refilling my bucket. Downtime for me has to be long enough that I'm confident I'll be better and ready by the time the next thing happens. When my schedule gets heavy, downtime isn't always as effective because I am stressed and questioning if I'm going to be ready before the next thing on my schedule.

With all this in mind, it's very important for me to know and follow a plan. Scheduling is crucial. Downtime, whatever that entails for the particular person on the spectrum, has to be factored into the schedule. Meeting a friend to hang out in a social environment can actually be tiring because trying to successfully carry on a conversation takes a huge amount of energy. You may not see that when interacting with me, but it is there, so I may have to spend as much time to recover from what people consider a leisure activity as from a work activity. That often doesn't make sense to people, and it can seem very unusual which activities are stressful for the person on the spectrum and how he recovers from them. Mental energy is drained during challenges for anyone and is very tiring; and we are almost always being challenged mentally to keep an interaction from going off track due to something we didn't pick up or misunderstood. Making a schedule that allows for plentiful recovery time is essential.

CHAPTER 9
FAMILY

"True understanding, which is more than just awareness, is critical. Paul writes in a way that explains his experiences and thoughts without any blame, excuses or attempts to elicit sympathy. The addition of Mom and Dad comments provide insight into the difficulties and confusion experienced by parents and other loved ones. This book is a much-needed addition to the body of literature concerning Autism."

Lyn Hassenboehler, MSW, LCSW, Clinical Social Worker

The Family Bond — I Don't Get It

What makes a family special? Why do I treat these people differently than other people? Why is a parent an authority in my life? Why do they get to tell me what to do? For those of us on the spectrum, the answers to those questions aren't necessarily obvious or intuitive, and not being able to understand how and why most people would answer those questions can result in creating a lot of friction in the family. On top of that, we don't always have the same emotional attachment with the rest of the family to offset the friction.

A lot of things in a family are done because "family" is a reason to do them, but that doesn't always make sense to me. The family "eats together at six o'clock," "visits our aunt in town once a month," "is Methodist and goes to church on Sunday mornings," etc. I wonder who created the idea that "the family" is the reason to do things like that. I don't understand or have an answer, but it can be a problem or confusing for those of us on the spectrum when we just don't get it.

I think I love and appreciate my family, but in a different way than most people do. I appreciate my family because they help me and are an important part of my life. My family appreciates me because I'm family. To me, family is just the people around me, and I don't have the same bonds with them as they expect. When they need me to go out of my way to help them, I will if it seems reasonable or appropriate. If not, I don't see why it's still expected of me or why they get so upset if I don't want to do it.

Our culture expects strong family ties and the expectation that children act as a part of the family. It can cause confusion or be disappointing to people when families with an autistic member aren't as strong as culture would expect them to be. Some of us on the spectrum may not grasp what it means to be a family member and the importance of family obligations, which is very difficult for the parents of a child on the spectrum to understand. It's the same sort of frustration for those of us on the spectrum. My family has expectations of me and I have of them, but neither is being met because we both have a different mental grasp or interpretation of what this relationship actually means and how it should work.

For me, without the natural intuitive ties and bonds to my family, there are a lot of expectations that surprise me. Imagine if someone had expectations of you that seemed nonsensical. Perhaps your spouse expected that every time they work in the yard, you should immediately start cleaning the house. If you didn't know of this expectation you were intuitively obligated to do, both of you would be frustrated. That's how I feel when faced with family obligations that are never explained to me. A family with autism requires a lot more direct communication than other families to try to help with this, because as I see it, being a family member isn't voluntary but comes with a lot of unsaid expectations and obligations.

With autism, since we don't have that family cultural connection to understand why it's good to do certain things, the expectations on us can feel like random demands. It can be very hard to sort that out. I don't know how the typical kid thinks of it, but I assume he feels he's asked to do a lot but accepts it because of this culturally implied familial tie to his parents.

My family consists of my mom, dad, and brother. Our personalities are different, and we don't have the same interests or the same ways to connect, but we are family. While I do care for them, it's difficult for me to define what it means to be attached to my family.

Families with someone on the autism spectrum have to work very hard at communicating. Communications easily break down if I'm not showing my commitment to the family and what it means to be in a family, or they're not showing me what I'm looking for in a family. Your child with autism still loves you but doesn't express it the same way you do. What love means to him may be different than what love means to you. Gary D. Chapman's book, *The 5 Love Languages*, talks about different ways people internalize genuine expressions of love. Some of those ways may sound hollow to you because it differs from the way you normally express or internalize love. Our culture expects familial love to cause us to engage in the social ways a family expresses these feelings, but when someone doesn't grasp those things or it's just not part of how they interpret the world, the family may see the lack of those social gestures as a lack of love. I want to make clear that when you have a child with autism, it does not mean he doesn't love you. Expressing it is his challenge.

These challenges cause much frustration for parents and siblings as well as those of us on the spectrum. As a child, when things went wrong, I would deal with it by getting away and staying in my room until I felt it was over or I could deal with what was going on. I learned to stay as long as I needed in order to feel better about everything and everybody.

 ## Teaching Values

Family plays a big role in communicating values. Many times values are things we sort of see as "common sense," but the reason for certain values is not always obvious to me. Rarely does anyone say why this is a good value or why it is important in their mind. Though some values (like not hurting other people) are obvious, others are much more subtle because they come from religious or cultural teaching. It helps me if my family tells me why they think a certain value is important and then we can discuss it.

A lot of my values are not because I was told them, but because I agree with them based on my experience in the world. In some cases, someone may have taught me something but my experiences taught me to push it away. When someone sees the world in almost a completely different way than those of us on the spectrum, the way values grow and develop can be very different from the rest of the family. If you are a parent trying to raise a child on the autism spectrum, you may teach certain values but the child may not display them the same way other children might. Your child may end up with some of the same values or they may not. How they interpret and act upon those values can be very different from what you expect.

The idea of parental authority and obeying your parents comes to mind, as it's a cultural value. Who sits down and talks to a child about why he should obey his parents? For parents of children on the spectrum, it works better when you make time to explain to the child that parents have more experience, have been through these things before, and because they love you they are giving you guidance in your best interests until you have the needed life experience and have developed your own good decision-making processes.

As children growing up, we are exposed to many things that might indicate the importance of respecting your family and others, via TV, books, the classroom, and from other children's interactions with their own parents. For us on the spectrum, it doesn't soak in the same way and we may not pick up certain values, which can cause a lot of frustration on both sides. Parents love the child and believe he will understand the message and reasoning that he should respect his parents. If he doesn't, they will think he rejected them rather than he never fully understood the message in the first place. The parent sees an intentional action of knowing "better" and repeating the offending action, rather than a misunderstanding.

Many times parents feel it's very important to raise their child like they were raised. You might have lived in a Christian household and want your child to have a Christian faith, or maybe you lived in a home where you were taught the value of hard work with chores and in return were provided with an allowance. You believe teaching these concepts are a necessary part of raising your child, but maybe an allowance doesn't work for your child on the spectrum, or trying to instill your faith in that child is not being grasped. If they can't internalize this value in the same way you do, you may need to look at other ways for them to learn the same lessons.

If taking your child to church doesn't work well, perhaps help him one-on-one with reading the Bible and understanding what the lessons, parables, or stories are trying to teach him. Look at how to apply these concepts to his everyday life. Part of teaching a child on the spectrum is stepping away from the way you've learned yourself and letting go of the idea that there is only one right way to do it. Be creative, and ask yourself, "What are we trying to accomplish?" This same thinking applies to schoolwork.

A person on the spectrum can find their own emotional attachments to many things like religion, people, etc. It may not be in the same way others do, but it does happen. I have definitely met a number of people on the spectrum who have had this experience. Once again it is based upon the perception of the individual. Understanding is more likely to occur for the person on the spectrum when the subject is presented one-on-one. While it may take more time, more creativity, and possibly a lot more effort, the result will be rewarding. A one-on-one setting helps the person on the spectrum make more progress in many areas of life. It may require repetition, more time, and most of all patience, but it works well for many of us.

CHAPTER 10
FRIENDSHIP

"Being different is about finding your unique talent and working with that talent to contribute to the greater community. Paul Louden is an individual with autism who has the ability to see and communicate truth and genuineness with a keen introspect of the behaviors of others."

Rev. Vita P. Como, M. Div., Head of the Monarch School and Institute in Houston

 **What is a Friend?**

I use the term "friendship" with a different meaning than most people. I have people I share interests with and those interests bring us together, but the way I share those interests is different from the way most people would. The things we do or talk about as well as how often we see each other are very different from the way most people interact.

Sometimes a neurotypical individual connects with someone he does not have a shared interest in, but finds that he enjoys just listening to the other person talk. This person may make him laugh, and he enjoys time with them. He does not look at someone and ask himself, "Why do I want to be friends with this person?" He is around that person and friendship happens naturally if they are compatible. The autistic child does not just grow into this understanding of friendship. Wanting friends is something that comes naturally to everyone including those of us on the spectrum. By observing people around me, I know I am missing how to make friends and would have liked someone to teach me when I was younger, but we can't learn it from just anyone who knows how to make a friend. We need someone who has a special insight with an in-depth view of where we are and can explain it in a way we can grasp it.

If your child is not making friends, as a parent you may talk to him about the mechanics of friendship, such as how to be nice or how to wait your turn, but you don't really talk about the "why" of friendships. What is friendship? How is friendship defined by you? Can you come up with a solid definition to teach someone? Friendship is something that is so common that as children we just naturally make friends in social groups. When someone doesn't have those social instincts but is expected to, people on the outside are not really able to recognize what is going on or why it is not happening in a typical way.

Friends are few and far between for people on the spectrum, and friendship can be very difficult. I have friends, but holding on to them can become an issue and be difficult. Talking to a friend can often result in a misunderstanding that breeds frustration. Usually I try to walk away when we reach the point when things are not being understood. Sometimes my friend will want to patch things up, but I often believe any attempts I make could work out poorly. I am not able to communicate my thoughts and could likely only make the issue worse. In the past, I have often drifted away from friends when this happens and it is very difficult to handle.

The turmoil of trying to have a friend is very difficult to deal with. I don't really talk very much with friends about most of the problems I have because it is really hard to explain things. If I need to cancel our plans because I am too anxious, I try to say as little about it as possible. I'll say, "I'm having a bad day, and I can't hang out with you today," and leave it at that. I have found that if I say I'm really anxious today, the response may be, "Well, wouldn't getting out of the house and hanging with someone help you?" This starts a conversation wherein I try to explain the way my brain works, and my friend thinks I am trying to make excuses to avoid them. Sometimes they may try to give me sympathy about the problem, and though sympathy does not really help in maintaining my friendship, it is a listening ear. I am actually trying to be thoughtful of the other person so he does not have to experience what I am going through at that time.

To me, the biggest part of friendship is trust. The friends I've stayed closest with are the friends who I got to the point of understanding well. Even though they might occasionally behave in ways that I don't like, I know what kind of things they're likely to do. By my understanding of them, these situations have a much smaller impact on me. There are friends who are willing to understand that I have these challenges, and to take into mind that if I cancel an appointment at the last minute, it is a serious thing. They know I am not writing them off. A large part of it is they trust me now. Finding friends who understand that you need time alone can help you by not making you feel guilty about having to cancel. These are the friends you want.

Mom's Story

When Paul turned eight, I wanted to give him a birthday party. I asked him who he wanted to invite. He named no one. When I asked him for some names of kids in his class, he couldn't name a single child.

 ## Sarcasm

Sarcasm is something that a lot of high-functioning individuals on the autism spectrum talk about that was challenging for them, especially during their grade school and middle school years. Someone may sarcastically say, "Great job man," but mean, "You did a terrible job." A lot of people on the spectrum might figure out the true meaning, but likely have to think about it consciously and may not immediately get it.

Those of us on the spectrum learn pretty quickly not to take sarcasm literally, but because it's a conscious process for us to rationalize sarcasm we may not react immediately. If we did a poor job responding, it may cause confusion for a few minutes. We may not realize if someone is making fun of us. As a result, a person on the spectrum faces a dismal challenge to try to stay in the mainstream with the other kids.

Some kinds of mild teasing and friendly sarcasm that are supposed to be positive things can be interpreted as something else, like people are seriously making fun of you. These things make teasing hard to interpret and sarcasm hard to understand. The person on the spectrum either misses it entirely or takes longer than anyone else to get it. It's obvious to other kids that one kid is acting different, and it helps create that feeling of separation and isolation common to a child on the spectrum. The higher functioning the child on the spectrum is, the more the child notices something is different and he doesn't understand what it is or how to handle it.

Over time, I have learned usually that tone of voice is a clue to sarcasm. That may seem obvious to you, but as you know, detecting and understanding tone of voice is not easy or natural for us. Frequently, sarcasm can also be in an email or online instant message, and without vocal cues at all, we have to find clues in the context. Sometimes people think the child on the spectrum is stupid or slow since they aren't catching on to the sarcasm. It can be age thirteen or later when those of us on the spectrum start to catch on. Sarcasm is one of those challenges that particularly stands out. We may not know when we are being teased or may feel we're being made fun of when it's just good-natured teasing or joking. The bottom line is our difficulty with understanding sarcasm is a challenge and deterrent in building relationships of any kind, can make socializing very challenging, and can make building friendships very difficult.

CHAPTER 11
SCHOOL

"As a former high school teacher, I had students that, looking back, were likely on the spectrum, and they had a hard time with their peers and their teachers. If I had the insights from this book, I would have been a better teacher for those children and could have helped them more effectively in school. I learned one really important thing from this book... it's not personal, it's just data. Responses from people on the spectrum can easily be misunderstood, but understanding how they process data and how they respond in such black-and-white manners is helpful to understand that their responses are not meant to be disrespectful or rude, rather it is just a response to data. This is much easier to understand now."

Mark Cheverton, New York Times bestselling author of the Gameknight999 Minecraft series.

School Can Be Tough

My mom made sure I had plenty of books from a very early age. I began reading at age two so when I started school a few years later I was ahead in many ways—but not socially. I never understood that part of our school experience was being around other students and learning to interact with each other, even through high school. In the early grades, I did fine in school but had issues because I would often spot textbook errors or mistakes the teacher made and point them out. This was often frustrating or embarrassing to the teacher but I had no idea of that.

As I approached fifth and sixth grade, I missed class often because of an upset stomach and we couldn't figure out why. I felt unwell due to frustration and anxiety, and wasn't picking up on hints about what would be on the test and wasn't seeing how the social issues of school were handled. It's not unusual for those of us on the spectrum to experience these kinds of issues. I began to feel that learning would be easier by myself, but I had to go to school. Learning on my own individually or at home would have been less stress than dealing with the social side of the classroom.

On top of the social issues, oftentimes I found myself bored and frustrated because I already knew the information, and it wasn't being taught in a way I expected. By the time I'd reached sixth grade, teachers were frequently upset because I didn't do homework. At times my parents insisted I do it, but I still often didn't turn it in. I didn't grasp why it was so important to the teacher that I do my homework if I understood the material. I didn't understand that we weren't just studying topics, but I needed to do work on the topic to prove my understanding.

Even as I got older, I would occasionally point out a mistake the teacher made or an error in the textbook. I learned not to do it often, but it still frustrated me. I had no emotional empathy or control about these issues, nor could I comprehend or understand the appropriate or respectful way to raise my concerns.

In spite of my difficulties, I definitely learned while I was in school. I wasn't very good at interacting with others, but I tested fairly well in my classes for the most part, and also did well on the SAT. I was just one question shy of a perfect SAT score in my senior year, but that same year my GPA was barely high enough for me to graduate. That made no sense to anyone, and frustrated both the teachers and my parents. A common comment on my report card over the years was "Not working at his potential." As you can imagine, it was depressing to "have the potential" but not be succeeding and be unaware as to why.

If It's Implied — I Probably Won't Get It

I did not understand the concept of the teachers having authority, or that a student not doing his homework is disrespectful. I did have respect for teachers, but rather than respect for their authority, it was respect that when they taught me something it would be accurate. I'm sure I was always seen as a troublemaker because they didn't understand how I felt or could relate to what I was really thinking. At the time, I felt like I didn't have a place in school, but I know now that I did. Parents and teachers will tell you that the purpose of school is to learn, but it didn't feel like that to me as I kept missing the implied structure of a school environment.

Even as I've gotten older, it doesn't get much easier. There's a significant difference between consciously knowing something and really integrating it. I know what my challenges are but that doesn't necessarily make it easier to deal with them, though it does give me an advantage over where I was before I gained an understanding of autism. A person can be in a wheelchair and know why they are in this situation but it doesn't make the stairs any easier. Knowing your condition is very different from having a solution to the problem.

Those of us on the spectrum are not likely to just pick up things we see or hear. This is a fairly common issue, and most of the time there's a passive system for grasping instructions. What needs to be done must be presented with clarity, and laying out the boundaries in any setting, but especially school, is very important. It must be clearly written who the rule applies to and what the person must do. If a rule doesn't apply to teachers, then it must say it doesn't apply to them, as the person on the spectrum will likely not understand the implication the rule doesn't apply to teachers. It can be made clear by saying something like "only students must..."

This problem with implied rules can crop up in many kinds of situations. A dress code is a perfect example. It may seem very obvious to most people that the dress code applies only to students and not teachers, but it is not obvious to most on the spectrum. The assumption could be if the student can make B's in his classes, he should be able to pick up on simple instructions. He might even be accused of trying to pick a fight, but it's really a different kind of thought process that picks up implications versus explicit instructions. Writing simple, direct rules with no room for assumptions can help parents and teachers reach the person on the spectrum. Clarity is essential for whatever application is necessary. Remember, we view instructions in black and white.

I would like to point out that autism itself does not indicate intelligence delay of any sort. Instead, it indicates the person has challenges taking in information and absorbing it in the same context as other people. Those of us on the spectrum often learn at a regular rate, without interference from an additional learning disability.

One of the big concerns of autism is that the individual may not learn what you expect them to learn. Values you consider important and necessary should be taught early so the child has time to learn your expectations and concerns before other things interfere. It's really not a matter of timing; it's more developing the right way. Teaching can begin when you feel ready and they're ready to learn.

CHAPTER 12
ROMANCE

It's Not Like the Movies

When I was in high school, I saw other kids dating and watched romantic relationships on television and in movies. I was trying to be "normal," so I figured I should be dating as well. I didn't really know how or why, or even understand what a relationship was supposed to be. I didn't have the necessary tools to understand the rights and wrongs of relationships.

TV shows and movies marketed for teens and young adults often contain a romance subplot, and the guy usually ends up with the girl in the end. Very rarely is a real relationship or real romance depicted. Stories showing a guy trying to get a girl indicate the only really important thing is persistence: the guy never stops trying until the girl agrees to go out with him, they fall in love, and then everything's okay.

As a young adult on the spectrum trying to understand this, I began thinking this is the way it must be. As no one sat me down and talked to me about what it means to have a girlfriend, how to date, or how to meet and talk to girls, I needed preparation before entering this part of life. If I had understood what it means to have a relationship and knew what's wrong with television romances it would have been a big help.

I am at the point now where I'm able to work this out, but it took me a long time. I still have many areas where I'm uncertain, but at least I recognize media relationships are a bad starting point for the real world. I have also figured out that relationships are not supposed to be anything specific and I can't make them happen, with persistence or otherwise.

Dating

How do you encourage the person on the spectrum when you see he or she obviously likes someone? First, don't try to tell them too many absolutes, as they will take those absolutes as irrefutable fact. Instead, provide opportunities for them to figure out their own answers. If you see them interested in someone, you might try leading questions like, "Why are you interested in her?" or "Why do you want to date someone right now?" Give them the opportunity to consider it and maybe write an occasional prompter. The object is to help them come up with their own idea of what dating is.

If they give answers like "Well, that's what I'm supposed to do, right?" then challenge any ideas coming from entertainment media. Don't try to give them an answer as much as provide the opportunity to exercise skills made weaker by autism. You don't want to cause them to consciously do what should happen unconsciously.

Whatever you tell them, they are probably going to take as the absolute truth. For example, if you tell your daughter how you met your husband and how the relationship unfolded, she might think she needs to copy what you did. Maybe, at age twenty-two, you went to a dance in another town and met a young man. She might think, "Okay, I'm supposed to meet a guy at a dance when I'm twenty-two." She wonders, "Why are there no dances to meet people? What if I'm twenty-three and I haven't met someone?" She may take what you say literally or think finding someone has to happen in a specific way.

It's good to point out some people may get into a relationship when they're young, but it's also okay to wait a while. Make sure he or she understands there's not a strict way it's supposed to happen. There's an impulse or feeling guiding you in finding some-one that you want to date, and figuring out who you like and who you want to have a relationship with is an incredibly personal thing. People on the spectrum can have a relationship, but it's not going to be the same as we see on television. If you start trying to have those kinds of relationships, it's not going to work out well.

If someone isn't sure about the kind of person he should be dating, talk to him about the idea that dating isn't essential. He may learn that he can find what he's looking for through friendship, too. Until he comes up with his own reason for wanting to date, there's not much point in it. It's really important to have your own motivation for a relationship because that's how you decide if it's working or not. How you construct a healthy relationship in general is not about following a specific set of guidelines learned from a book or a movie, it's about a connection between two people.

 ## Dating Expectations — We May Need Some Guidance

Successful dating depends upon your expectations. People on the autism spectrum cannot be very flexible so success depends upon limiting expectations. I grew up on Archie comics so my perception of dates was to give the girl a flower, take her to dinner, and so on. By the time I was in high school, I learned that showing up with a flower wasn't really normal. The challenge was my expectation of dating as being structured, and this was what you were supposed to do rather than just showing up and getting together. A lot of this issue ties into one of the biggest challenges in autism—trying to develop flexibility.

If you don't have the flexibility, then the best thing to do is match expectations beforehand. This is another time that parents might want to talk about what dates are, how dates are with two people, and finding out what the other person likes to do. Explain about making sure that what you do also incorporates what the other person likes to do. It's all about managing your expectations when you can't have the flexibility needed.

When a guy on the spectrum discovers the girl he likes is not interested, he may start pestering her to find out why. He may have the impression that relationships fail because there's something in the way, and may pursue finding out what he can fix. Without a good idea of what a relationship is, it's very hard to handle. The most important part a parent can play is trying to get information to their child BEFORE there's a chance for something to go wrong. Provide a different view of a relationship, something more real than what's depicted in media. People typically pick up from their family and friends how a normal relationship works, but people on the spectrum don't learn from the social behavior of those around us.

Special Relationships are Possible

For people on the spectrum having a special relationship with another person, I think you absolutely need to tell the person about your autism before getting too far into it. The diagnosis doesn't make anything worse. The other person may get angry because you didn't tell them, or if you just got diagnosed they might be terrified of it because they are hearing it for the first time.

Remind them, "You've been dating me for this long and I'm still the exact same person I was before I ever said the word autism to you. I have not changed in any way. I am exactly who I was five minutes ago, and I will still be the same person. I have grown over the last year and will continue growing. Now that we know about the autism diagnosis, maybe you can help guide me in the direction that helps us as a couple."

Having the diagnosis allows us to grow and improve our relationships. Whatever reason you didn't reveal it, or whenever you do, you can always say, "I was diagnosed, and I'm telling you about it now. I was autistic the day I was born, and I'm the same person."

Relationships are difficult even for average people, but there are also special challenges for people on the autism spectrum. At the same time, there may be some advantages. Some people on the spectrum may react to certain things differently or possibly even better. Every person is different.

Yes, relationships are possible. There are people on the autism spectrum who are married and raising children. Their autism does create challenges and differences. Especially for the high-functioning people on the spectrum, these are things that you can work around. It's going to vary from person to person, but there's no reason to rule marriage out. I wouldn't want to discourage marriage, even though some might need encouragement to wait until they've had some more life experiences. Overall, autism is not a reason to avoid having relationships.

Inside every autistic person there are the same general needs for connection and interaction that a typical person has. The person on the spectrum may express it differently, and these expressions may vary. Typically, at some point he is going to want to make friends. At some point he may want a romantic relationship. The timing for these connections can be very different than expected.

When it comes to special relationships, challenges exist, but they do not change the great person inside. It's just a matter for those of us on the spectrum to be able to accept the challenge and to recognize the potential outcomes, which may work out or may not. We also have to recognize that not everyone we date is going to be able to handle the challenge of dating someone with autism. This can be hard to deal with when you thought another person really cared for you. Realizing autism is preventing you from having this particular relationship can be very hard to deal with.

Learning to walk away from a relationship is a tough lesson for anyone, particularly those on the spectrum. Some people, businesses, family members, and potential significant others cannot deal with it. Situations are going to arise where autism gets in the way of things you want to do in your life. Autism is a barrier, but we are all working to improve ourselves and make our lives better. We have to learn not to let barriers and setbacks related to autism stop or destroy us.

CHAPTER 13
WORK

"Paul's insights are profound, and he outlines all aspects of various life skills. Whether one works or lives with people with autism, all will benefit from learning what Paul is teaching."

Karen Kabaki-Sisto, M.S. CCC-SLP,
is an autism communication expert

The unemployment rate for people on the spectrum is huge and has been quoted at anywhere from 80% to 97% unemployed. You may be surprised to learn this holds true for high-functioning people on the spectrum as well. For those who are employed, the average salary is near minimum wage and far below the median expected for the education level.

It is a huge challenge for most of us on the spectrum to hold a job. It demands a combination of work and social skills. In my experience, you don't have to be good friends with those you work with, but you have to stay in good standing with them socially and emotionally. For someone on the spectrum, that is incredibly challenging. Who explains that to you? We are supposed to understand intuitively because it comes so naturally to average people, but we would be better off having it explained to us.

When I first started working, I thought a job should require only what the job description says. When things went badly for me at a job due to social situations, it was hard for me to not be resentful because we are hired to do a job and it shouldn't matter what others think of me as long as I am doing the job correctly. Being friendly and inviting is very challenging for many of us.

There are many other factors that can make holding a job difficult for those on the spectrum. The work environment may be too noisy, or traveling to work can be too stressful because of the crowds. Sudden changes in routine are difficult to handle for us as well. Also very important, decision-making on how complete to do the job is very challenging for us. Knowing when "good enough" is enough is very hard for us to grasp. Making judgments of time constraints versus quality may take a long time for us to learn and vary from job to job.

However, many of our strengths are positives to employers. Those of us on the spectrum often give a lot of attention to detail and may have intense focus. Jobs that seem unattractive to others because of their repetitive nature may be very appealing for individuals on the spectrum.

I have a hard time finding motivation within myself, even now. While I'm capable of doing many things, some of the internal processes of motivation seem missing. Each person on the spectrum may be different, but I've found I tend to need a few things to work well and I rarely do well on my own. I don't need someone doing the task with me, but I do need someone to occasionally re-focus me on the task. If it's a task I've chosen to do, such as a proj-ect I want to complete, that often means listening to me talking about it, and helping to direct my enthusiasm to action. If it's a task I don't want to do, it's often about setting starting times so that I can begin work. In both cases, I also have a hard time resuming work if I stop. This is true of small breaks, but especially true of failures. In both cases, I need someone who can kick-start the process again. With a little help in these ways, once I'm working on a task I can often do it with a surprising amount of focus and energy.

CHAPTER 14
THERAPY

"The book is great. "Behind the Locked Door"
is not just a book for families affected by the
challenges of autism. It is a must-read for all
health care professionals. It opens the veil
and reveals to us how autism is experienced
by our patients and their families.
It has given me critical insight into
the disorder and will help me provide
more compassionate care to my patients
and their families."

Kelley Carroll, MD, Family Physician

Focus on Quality of Life

When trying to treat or help those of us on the autism spectrum, there are two major goals in my view, and they are both equally important. First, which is most commonly addressed, is to improve on the weaknesses that the person has in interacting with other people. The other goal is improving "quality of life." Improving quality of life takes into account that those of us on the spectrum will never be completely typical. We want to work on improving ourselves but we also need to accept there are long-term issues we face and put some focus on how to live a happy, healthy life with those issues. When looking for therapy, keep in mind that it needs to address both of these.

How does a therapist work effectively with a person on the spectrum? Since there is no cure or known cause, there is not a really good answer to that. There are a lot of different therapies and many people have different opinions of how effective those are. Any parent addressing autism therapy needs to keep in mind these two questions, "Will it help my child to get along in the world?" and "Will it help them feel better on their own?" When you talk to therapists, try to find out if the therapist cares about these questions and which, if any, they care about more. Listen to how the therapist is going to approach each of these. Parents know their child and should judge the right approach for themselves.

Therapy should be based upon the particular needs of the person with autism and the therapist should offer a strategy to meet these needs. A parent should see positive changes in their child to determine if the therapy is being effective, but don't rush. With therapy, the biggest goal is to not look at how fast you are moving forward but just that you are moving forward. No matter when you begin therapy, it's a long process, and for some it may be a lifetime. If the person with autism is happy and comfortable with their differences, and is able to keep those differences from interfering with their ability to have friends, a relationship if desired, a job, or a happy life, the goal has been reached.

There are different approaches and types of autism therapy. When looking for results, I believe it is important to differentiate if new behaviors are due to understanding versus mimicking. As an example, a person can memorize a math fact or the answer to question on a test, yet cannot solve the same problem with different numbers or understand why the answer for the question is true. They are not taught the tools to work backward to solve the answer. Memorizing is not the same as deeper understanding. People need to be taught from the ground up how all the pieces fit together rather than giving them just answers. In autism therapy, when working on issues with communication or emotions, it's often not treated this way.

When those of us on the spectrum are told to do something, we may ask "Why do I need to do this?" The answer quite often that we hear is "You're just supposed to do this," or "You do this to make people happy." When I follow this advice and it does not work out, I think "I can't make them happy; I don't understand why I need to make someone happy." People often attempt to offer help by saying what to do when we ask for help. I don't need to know what to do, what I really am asking is "what is my goal," and "why" do I want to make someone happy. If I understand the "why," then the explanations of how to do it make more sense to me.

Therapies that address certain specific situations work for the short term, but that does not offer understanding of what the real goal is. In situations where the script learned suddenly changes, perhaps a different setting or different response to a question, we may not recognize that it is very similar and don't know what to do. The world is too unpredictable to practice every scenario, and the gaps in understanding need to be found.

Many therapies depend on memorization. Often therapists will use flash cards with facial expressions or similar resources to show the person on the spectrum how to respond when someone approaches or talks to them. Again, a misunderstanding could occur if the situation practiced does not match the situation that the person on the spectrum finds themselves in. It is not that these therapies are inherently bad, it is just a case of autism being seen as a series of symptoms to address and in reality it is much deeper and more complicated.

That's not to say it isn't sometimes useful to address symptoms. If your child reacts to certain things by screaming, you are going to want to address the screaming problem in the short term even if you are not sure of the cause. A balanced approach is important. You want to look at easing symptoms, but you also want to understand what caused them. What was going on in the child's mind? If the cause is not addressed, new symptoms could crop up as the child develops his own answer to handle his situations.

A lot of adults with autism are still challenged by everyday life, even after therapy. Though therapy might aid in dealing with seventy to eighty percent of these issues, that is not enough to lead an anxiety-free life. One trap people fall in is the mistaken belief "What will make me happy, will make others happy." Additionally, parents often project their concept of a "good life" onto their children. This isn't inherently a bad thing; it produces a framework that a child can fill in and adapt to their own desires as their sense of self expands and they become a more independent human being. In the case of an individual with autism, we are less likely to push back against these ideas, but rather pursue them even at the cost of our own satisfaction. It's common to hear stories from high-functioning individuals who are distraught because they "should" have a girlfriend, and are pursuing one without even being able to answer why they want one.

To really address this, the parents, family, and support will have to focus on developing a sense of personal agency. The individual with autism needs to be wholly aware it's their life, and they can make decisions about how it should look and what its goals may be. A healthy life is your life, not the life someone else thinks you should live.

 ## There is No Timeline; Progress is Two Steps Forward and One Step Back

Therapy can be slow and takes time. There is no score and no set way to indicate your objective has been met. Ideally, a parent would be involved and continually communicating with the therapist about what is going on. The therapist should be recommending using different ways of communicating or trying to involve your child in more daily activities, like helping make dinner, fold clothes, etc. As a parent, you need to try to integrate your child more into your household and create situations that will help your child grow. You can use these times as opportunities to observe and decide if the therapy is constructive or not. If you don't know, you are not involved enough.

Even as an adult in therapy, I found that improvement is not that "cut-and-dried" and results did not come overnight. Progress is not easy to measure and it is a very gradual process. For me, a measure of therapy progress is for changes to be occurring without me noticing it. I shouldn't be constantly thinking about making eye contact, so if one day I just notice I'm making more eye contact without thinking about it, then I believe I'm making progress. When I gradually become comfortable doing a certain thing, it will seem natural and I won't notice it. One of the best feelings I have is when people around me make comments like "you seem to be getting along with people better" or "you seem less stressed." That's one of the best gauges I really have, and I've found if I pay too much attention to a goal or become too conscious of it, it tends to undermine my progress.

Of course there are always specific therapy goals with objectives you can work on as a parent, like wanting your child to dress himself. Those are concrete and objective. Setting a time to meet a developmental goal will not work as every person develops at their own speed. In addition, watching for that big goal can cause you to overlook the smaller but significant progress being made.

Whether it's a small child or an adult, the goal for any therapy is to help the person on the spectrum develop into a more competent, confident person who is less anxious or stressed about everyday life. This happens slowly and sometimes in a two steps forward and one step back process where the steps can take many months at times.

Anxiety and Depression

Dealing with anxiety and depression is a big challenge for us. As I've already shared, we react to certain situations in our own way and relate differently. We face increased stress and difficulty managing emotions, and have fewer skills for dealing with these problems. Without good support, it's easy to feel isolated and helpless.

A lot of the processes of working through depression and anxiety have to be handled differently for people on the spectrum. As we view the world and think about things in a different way than the average person, how we address these issues of anxiety and depression often needs to be different as well. Finding help becomes a real challenge. Frequently, for high functioning individuals, it becomes one of the primary challenges of our lives. We may feel we can handle our autism well enough to get by or to hold a job. It may not be the job we want, but it's a job. But there are still quality of life issues. We need to address the anxiety and depression that often comes to the forefront as these things are still getting in the way of having a good quality of life.

I personally had a difficult time finding a therapist I could work with. I met with one and talked with her for over an hour. She told me she didn't think she could help me because we would have to approach the problems from her perspective and method, and that wasn't going to work for me. My advice is to not accept it if a therapist says you have to do therapy their way without input or compromise. Find someone you are comfortable with and look for progress. It's okay to say, "Your methods may work but we need to come up with a way where I'm actually going to want to do them and be motivated."

Eventually I found a therapist to work with that worked well with me. She also suggested medications and although some didn't work well for me due to side effects, after some time I found a medication that was helpful in reducing the anxiety that permeates my life. I also found it helpful to address my approach to my own situation and how I think autism plays out in my life. As I've learned more about it and the challenges that come with it, I've had to rethink these challenges in new ways. As a result, they don't create as much anxiety and depression as they had in the past.

Dad's Story

Paul suffered from severe depression and anxiety as a young adult. When his mother and I visited him at his apartment when he was in his early twenties, all the lights would be very dim and the shades completely closed. He often went out only at night and knew all the places that were open twenty-four hours.

Mom's Story

I remember one time in high school, Paul was depressed. He told me he wasn't going to kill himself, but he wouldn't stop himself from dying either. We hoped when he went out on his own things would get better.

After high school he moved to Arizona to study video game programming. In the fall, his car broke down and he didn't tell us. He didn't know what to do about it. He couldn't drive to class so he quit school. We found out only when we didn't see a report card. By then, his car had been impounded for sitting in the parking lot without moving. He had gotten many notices to move the car, but didn't know what to do and didn't ask.

CHAPTER **15**
DISCLOSURE

"I was able to experience through Paul's stories the realities of being Autistic and how they impact your total character of life. To me, this is very different from your quality of life – the character of life is the broadest range of experiences and interactions. It is the universal part of being."

Jeff Lewis, Human Resources, Payroll & Facilities

I Have Autism — Who Do I Tell and When?

Who you tell, when, and how much you choose to say is what I'm referring to when I say "disclosure." A common question I'm asked is "Should I tell people about my autism diagnosis?" I think that's the wrong question. For me it's "When should I tell them?" I think disclosure in the long term is always positive. You may want to wait, and sometimes it may be a long time, but I believe in the long term it's always beneficial to tell people about it. There's more to gain than to lose.

There are two types of disclosure. There are parents who have a child on the spectrum and have to decide how to explain to the child he has autism. Also, there is a person who has his own diagnosis and is trying to decide when to tell other people about it. For parents the only advice I can offer is to pay attention to your child and explain when you think he is mature enough to understand the diagnosis information and use the information in a positive way.

It may be that once he understands the problem he can come up with ways to say, "Okay, now that I know about it and understand what my challenges are, I can start working on it." Perhaps it's when he starts to realize he's having difficulty with other people, and sees that it's more than just being awkward — that there's something dramatically wrong here. It's going to vary based upon where he is developmentally, in terms of emotional maturity, and what kind of personality he has. Look for an opportunity in your child's life when it can be revealed constructively.

When it comes to personal diagnosis and disclosure, it's very important to me that people see me as "Paul" who's on the spectrum rather than "that autistic guy" Paul. Sometimes people see the diagnosis of autism first and sometimes they see the person first. It's similar to getting to know someone over the Internet and then later finding out they're in a wheelchair. If you saw the wheelchair first, you may start thinking about, "Oh, I'm going to have to push them around," or, "How can we hang out together," as opposed to getting to know them first and worrying about that later.

When I meet someone for the first time, I want to get to know them before I tell them about being on the spectrum. I want them to know me as a person first. When I deal with people socially or in confidence, it shouldn't be relevant anyway. My goal is that it should not be relevant most of the time, but there are situations when it's going to create challenges, and in those cases, the earlier I reveal it the better.

It can be hard to know when it's time to reveal your autism. Recognizing social cues is often difficult. Is the other person going to be more comfortable or less comfortable knowing? It's helpful to have a close friend or family member who can help you judge those situations. Explain you've made a new friend and want to ask if they have any advice about sharing your diagnosis. Again, this is a very personal decision and very closely related to the situation at hand. I think the goal should always be to disclose your autism; it's just a matter of deciding how soon you want to disclose it.

 ## Disclosure is About Self-advocacy

When you decide to tell someone about your autism, there's really no way to know for certain how the person will respond. There are some people I've told who have said it really didn't matter that they would be my friend with or without the autism, while others don't believe autism is real. It's such a wide range of responses that I think the best preparation you can have is as much knowledge as possible about yourself, the disorder and how the disorder affects you.

I also think disclosure is about self-advocacy, and saying, "I have these challenges and I'm trying to deal in the most positive way I can." Once they know about my diagnosis and more about autism they may become less stressed or less challenged by inter-action with me. Education is the best thing we can do to strengthen ourselves for proper disclosures.

Sometimes it has been clear that there wasn't going to be any benefit in trying to explain or talk about it. Fortunately, that isn't typically the case, and so far, I haven't had a lot of challenges with it.

We don't have to fight every battle with those who genuinely don't believe in autism for those of us at the supposedly high-functioning end of the spectrum. I may say a little about it, talk to them later, or just distance myself from them. I don't necessarily tell random people about autism. Sometimes people want to know more, but you don't want to get caught up in it. I disclose only to the people I know I'm going to have repeated encounters with and think it's going to be important that they know.

Many are very curious about it. It doesn't seem to have the stigma it once had because there is more awareness and information about it now, and I've gotten a huge range of responses. When disclosing to the right people, it usually comes with a lot of questions. I find that having knowledge of the disorder helps answer questions that surprise me. The majority of people I've told have responded well because I have known them for years. Most people are going to be positive and reasonable, though there are skeptics around. The people who like to claim that it's a lack of discipline are always going to be there. It can be hard to recognize those people, and that's why it's good to already know those you want to offer disclosure.

Fear of judgment or criticism causes some parents to be afraid of telling others about their child's autism. Some people think the cause is related to poor parenting or unsafe behavior during pregnancy, and some think autism is caused by vaccines, but there's no solid evidence for any of that and much to the contrary. No mom or dad wants to be seen as a bad parent, regardless of how ill-informed others may be.

If a child is medium to high functioning, the parents may be reluctant to make others aware of it for fear of losing opportunities for their child. They may feel this puts their child at risk for a stigma that will make it more difficult for the child. Revealing your child is on the autism spectrum can make some parents feel very intimidated. I think the solution is to know as much as you can about autism so you can give other parents data to affirm your child is okay and is capable of playing with friends. While parents are dealing with the outside challenges of autism, the inside challenge of helping their autistic child is also there 24/7. In some situations it may end up not being worth the effort to deal with other parents and their lack of knowledge.

Dad's Story

Between the ages of eighteen and twenty-six, Paul did not go to the dentist. His mom and I were concerned, but we couldn't force him to go and the dentist experience had some very bad memories causing a lot of anxiety for Paul. When he eventually went, he had very bad tooth decay and had to have many teeth pulled and much work done. I told a friend at work about it who I had known well for many years. Later, I heard him making a sarcastic joke about it even though he knew Paul had autism. As a parent of a child with autism, these types of incidences are the reason we often don't want to talk about it and try to handle things internally. We find that the only people who can truly relate and understand are other parents of kids with autism.

CHAPTER 16
CONCLUSION

"This book leads to understanding and compassion. It helped me understand autism on a personal level. I understand the actions of people on the spectrum better and, in turn, understand how to improve communication with them. It painted a very textured picture of autism, with chapters on Flexibility, Appearance, Episodic Memory, Family and Romance, to name a few. You get a very good picture of what is like to live a life on the autism spectrum."

Luanne Pusateri, mother and mechanical engineer

It feels as if we've been working on this book forever. In all honesty, one could make a sound argument that it's been in production for thirty-three years. This book contains a lot of me—stories, lessons, thoughts, and ideas. Now you've read it, and you know many of the things I've learned during these years. Yet it's also just the surface of what's going on, and what's happening with autism in my personal case, let alone the hundreds of thousands of people affected by it in some way or another.

There are lessons in this book I struggle to put into action. There are things I've said I've learned that will surely prove wrong over the years, and new things I'll replace them with. I will make new friends, part with old ones, and find that the scope of my experiences is smaller than I imagined as new ideas and people pass through my life.

My life has broken down and been rebuilt constantly with new events. In many ways this is a usual event for people. New things happen and our ideas adapt. Often for those of us with autism it can be catastrophic. The breaking down of old ideas introduces uncertainty, and we often lean on experiences and knowledge and distrust, having to wing it or deal with uncertainty. I've had great people around me to help carry me through it, and get me back on track when I wasn't able to handle it myself.

I want you, the reader, to walk away with a few things in mind. This book isn't meant to arm you with specific tools. It's full of ideas and experiences of mine that you can use to craft your own tools. Some of them might be the same as mine, or those of my family. Others will be dramatically different. Some you'll discard, others will serve you well for the rest of your life.

You may be reading this book because you have autism, know someone with autism, because you're curious, or because someone has asked you to. No matter the specifics, your life is impacted by autism. The rates are high, and you almost certainly know someone on the spectrum or someone affected by someone on the spectrum.

These tools won't solve autism, but with a willingness to build and refine your response and a desire to be an ally, to listen and believe the experiences of the people around you, you can and will make a difference in someone's life. We are at the start of a journey across decades as we move from autism awareness to understanding, and eventually acceptance and integration. We've made great strides, but this journey is long, and I hope that reading this book has provided a few extra steps in your personal journey.

Thank you so much for reading, and I wish you the best of luck going forward from here.

Made in the USA
San Bernardino, CA
12 April 2018